A TRUE STORY

WHILE HE LAY DYING

BRUCE AND LARA MERZ

WITH DR. STEPHEN CRAWFORD, M.D. AND BISHOP TODD ATKINSON

Note: All details and events in this book are portrayed accurately as possible without addition or exaggeration, but some of the names have been changed to protect the privacy of individuals.

ISBN: 978-1-4600-0434-0
LSI Edition: 978-1-4600-0435-7
E-book ISBN: 978-1-4600-0436-4

(E-book available from the Kindle Store, KOBO and the iBooks Store)

Cataloguing data available from Library and Archives Canada

Cover design by Symetric Productions—www.spcan.com

Photos used by permission © Ryckman Photography

To view pictures, get additional information, or order more copies, please visit:

www.whilehelaydying.com

Essence Publishing is a Christian Book Publisher dedicated to furthering the work of Christ through the written word. For more information, contact: 20 Hanna Court, Belleville, Ontario, Canada K8P 5J2
Phone: 1-800-238-6376. Fax: (613) 962-3055
Email: info@essence-publishing.com
Web site: www.essence-publishing.com
www.essencebookstore.com

Dedication

With all our hearts and utmost gratitude, we dedicate this book to River of Life Church in Lethbridge, Alberta - an amazing local church and example of what the body of Christ can look like on Earth - and to the rest of the Church all over the world who walked so closely with us in unprecedented support, unified prayer, and compelling love. We'll continually be giving thanks to God for you for all eternity!

We also want to dedicate this book to our children! If you were the only ones to ever read this book, it would be entirely worth it. This story is part of your heritage, your legacy – and we look forward to the day when you're old enough to read it!

Table of Contents

Acknowledgments

First, thanks to all the hospital staff at Chinook Regional Hospital, who were a beautiful part of this story. We're so grateful for all your professionalism, skill and kindness toward our family and our friends (who cluttered your hospital for a while). Thank you!!

We also want to thank Todd and Steve for their unbelievable support to us during this ordeal, and for being part of this project! You guys are amazing and we're so proud to call you friends.

Special thanks also to Melody, Lara's brilliant mother who worked tirelessly in helping us edit the book, putting in countless hours of pouring over manuscripts, poignantly word-smithing our clumsy sentences, and graciously putting up with our incessant emails and questions. Thank you for believing in this project and putting your heart and soul into it to see it realized. It's as much your book, Melody, as it is ours.

Additional thanks to everyone who helped us in one way or another to complete the book, including Sherrill and Tim at *Essence Publishing* for all their wisdom, help, and expertise. Ryan and the rest of the gang at *Symetric Productions* for kindly donating their time and talent to design an awesome book cover. And Serene at *Sparkle Technologies* for creating a wonderful website for the book for free as well! Thank you all so much! We'd also like to thank those who let us use their house to write, who babysat, stopped by with smoothies, proof-read, gave advice, and more! All of your support and help made this entire project possible (and better), and made us feel loved as well. We feel incredibly blessed and grateful, indeed.

Almost last, we give our utmost thanks to our parents, who gifted us with a rich spiritual heritage, and to so many of our family and dear friends. You have supported us, laughed and wept with us, and believed in us. We would not be who we are without you.

Finally and most importantly, we want to thank God for - well, *everything*. He has literally blown us away with His goodness, kindness, and love! He never ceases to amaze us.

Thank you Father, for inviting us to be part of your family and for gifting us with this cool story. We hope we did it justice and that it makes you smile.

Foreword

Bruce and Lara first appeared on my radar when they visited Lethbridge, Alberta, Canada as they were considering moving from British Columbia. I knew when I met Bruce that he was a man that I would like to get to know, and the opportunity came a few months later as the Merz family packed up their goods and chattels in beautiful green B.C. and headed for the brown/often white semi-arid prairies of Southern Alberta.

I became their family doctor shortly after and was thrilled to confirm Lara's second baby was on the way and was slightly less delighted to remove Bruce's ingrown toenail. After I left family practice to become a full-time hospitalist at Chinook Regional Hospital in 2010, Lara and Bruce continued to be a genuine blessing in my life and in the lives of my family.

It was therefore a pleasure and a privilege to be able to stand with them, pray with them, laugh with them (until my sides hurt), and cry with them during the period in which this book is set. My wife and I marvelled at Lara's faith and openness through this whole experience and found it both humbling and inspirational. I have also witnessed the desire for integrity, medical accuracy, humility, and honesty and was asked to review both the relevant medical records and what has been recorded in this book. At Lara's request, I was, throughout this whole event, in regular contact with my medical and nursing colleagues who were involved in Bruce's care; I also eventually became his supervising physician. I can therefore assure you that this account of events is both medically and chronologically accurate.

While He Lay Dying

For those not familiar with the medical conditions mentioned in the chapters to come, I will explain some more after they tell their story. In the meantime, I hope you will catch a glimpse of the roller coaster that was the spring of 2013, as a tall, but to all intents and purposes, normal father of an average family, in a small and seemingly unimportant city, in a remote part of Canada, became the focus of truly international and arguably supernatural attention.

Dr. Stephen Crawford, MD (MBBS, BSc)

Jesus trusted His Father and gave Himself over to death on the cross.
Then followed a long Friday night and a long Saturday...
And while He lay in the grave, His followers asked,
"What was that all about?"

For some of you it's been a long wait...
Something died years ago.
Some part of your faith died.
Some part of your hope died.
Some promise you were holding onto died.
We cannot raise ourselves out of that...
But we've got a Father who is able to.

Bishop Todd Atkinson
Easter Sunday, 2013

Part One
Lara

Chapter One

A mazing. It's amazing how often God blesses us simply because He loves us.

It took me a long time to understand this. I thought there needed to be greater purpose for God to act other than the fact that He just loves me. I used to try to convince God that if He made something good happen in a bad situation or healed me of whatever ailment was afflicting me, then perhaps so-and-so would be impressed and come to know Him. I never knew that all He wanted was for me to realize that if I were the *only* person touched it would be worth it to Him because of His profound love for *me*. I am reason enough. So are you.

The ironic thing is that what I have learned about God came after I quit trying to convince Him to do miracles for me for the sake of reaching the whole world. Now that I am just accepting His love, I am realizing that the very miracles that He has done for me are, in fact, impacting the world.

My life has seen little miracles and big miracles—God moments. I suppose that is why I feel an urge to share what I have seen and experienced.

I am not a writer. I am not a theologian. I am not a preacher. I am a wife and a mother, but more than that, I am a child of God. This is not a seminary textbook. This is my story—our story—and I write this with the sole purpose of glorifying my Father in heaven for what He has done in my life and the lives of my family and for what he is doing in the body of Christ—the Church with a capital C.[1]

A little bit of history

I suppose "God moments" have been evident my whole life, but I'll begin with the part of this story that started on Thanksgiving Day, 2006.

I was 26, single, and devastated. A relationship that had promised to lead to marriage was over, and I finally had to admit it. That night after I checked the locked doors and dressed in a worn t-shirt and warm sweat pants, I climbed into my bed. I lay in the dark feeling like God answered other people's prayers—He just didn't answer mine. But this hurt so bad. I was tempted to call some friends and ask them to pray that God would heal my broken heart and allow me to move on. Wondering if I would ever recover from the heartache I was feeling or if loving again was even worth it, I fell asleep with tears soaking into my pillow.

A few hours later I suddenly awoke and sat bolt upright in my bed. What happened next was like watching a movie. I began to remember prayer after answered prayer, literally hundreds of answered prayers spanning over a decade. It was like the Lord was reminding me of years of answered prayers—little prayers, big prayers, and things that I had long forgotten.

One of them was praying for my mom as she fumbled around on the piano while accompanying her singing students at their year-end recital. My mom is usually a good pianist, and it wasn't like her to have so much trouble playing, so I prayed God would help her, and He did. After the last people left, I stayed behind to help her tidy up, and she asked me, "Were you praying or something? That was so incredible! I was messing up so much and getting more and more flustered when all of a sudden I felt peace. I realized my fingers were automatically

---

[1] By Church with a capital C, I mean the church universal, rather than just a local congregation; that is, Christ's Body on Earth, which includes all Christians everywhere.

finding the right notes without effort. I felt like I hardly needed to look at the music!"

I had forgotten about that.

As I was watching nearly a hundred similar memories play on the screen in my mind, the Lord showed me the reason I didn't think He answered my prayers. It was simply because I was not thankful when He did. Without an attitude of thanksgiving, those memories were lost to me. He continued to answer my prayers despite my ungratefulness, but I was so in the habit of asking and asking and then moving on to the next dramatic thing that I never stopped to realize that He had answered the previous prayer. That night the Lord taught me something that has changed my spiritual walk forever: thankfulness is a key to seeing breakthroughs in our lives.

Philippians 4:4-9 says this:

"Rejoice in the Lord always. I will say it again: Rejoice! Let your gentleness be evident to all. The Lord is near. Do not be anxious about anything, but in every situation, by prayer and petition, *with thanksgiving*, present your requests to God. And the peace of God, which transcends all understanding, will guard your hearts and your minds in Christ Jesus. Finally, brothers and sisters, whatever is true, whatever is noble, whatever is right, whatever is pure, whatever is lovely, whatever is admirable—if anything is excellent or praiseworthy—think about such things. Whatever you have learned or received or heard from me, or seen in me—put it into practice. And the God of peace will be with you" (emphasis added).

I used to pray this out loud before I went to sleep whenever I felt anxious about something. No word of a lie though, I always skipped the words "with thanksgiving." I didn't even know they were in there until that night! I had recited the verse wrong all these years. In fact, the more I looked, the more I saw that verses about prayer were often linked with thanksgiving:

"Devote yourselves to *prayer*, being watchful and *thankful*" (Colossians 4:2, emphasis added).

While He Lay Dying

"Rejoice always, *pray* continually, *give thanks* in all circumstances; for this is God's will for you in Christ Jesus." (1 Thessalonians 5:16-18, emphasis added.)

"I have not stopped giving *thanks* for you, remembering you in my *prayers*." (Ephesians 1:16, emphasis added.)

"I urge, then, first of all, that petitions, *prayers, intercession* and *thanksgiving* be made for all people" (1 Timothy 2:1, emphasis added)

That night as I began to sift through those memories, the Lord spoke loudly in my spirit, "Time to give thanks, Lara!" So, I sat there, and for an hour I thanked Him for all of those forgotten prayers and their answers.

Then He told me to do something even harder. He told me to look into my present heartbreak (I was a mess on the inside at the time) and to give thanks for things *within* that situation.

Sometimes it is easy to give thanks for the roof over our head, for loving family members, or for food in the fridge, but to be thankful in the places of pain? *Are you serious, Lord?* This is truly where the breakthrough happened for me. I began to weep and thank the Lord for my tears because they meant my heart was still soft. I thanked Him for brokenness that showed that I was capable of loving deeply. My prayer time went on for hours. I wasn't giving thanks for being treated poorly but rather for the character it was producing in me, for God's evident and loving embrace, and the many more intricacies of His intentions that quickly became apparent to me. I was visiting places of pain and more pain, yet every time I gave thanks I was able to see something beautiful in myself and in the Lord—the way He carried me, rescued me, and held me. It changed my perspective entirely. When I focused on what was noble, right, pure, and lovely and gave thanks to God for those things, my perspective changed! Hope and faith came rushing in.

I was weeping hard with my face resting on my Bible, when I sensed the Lord telling me to lift up my head. When I finally did, I saw that my tears had stained these words in Isaiah 62:4:

"No longer will they call you Deserted, or name your land Desolate. But you will be called Hephzibah [My delight is in her], and your land Beulah [married]; for the LORD will take delight in you, and your land will be married."

I realize the verse in context was directed to another audience, but the Lord used it to speak to me at that moment. My spirit filled with more faith than I had ever experienced! I knew that I knew, that I knew that He was speaking to me and that I would be married. This may seem trivial to some, but those who have waited and longed for their soul mate for years will understand what an encouraging word that can be! I asked Him again and again if I would be married, and He said in my spirit, "Yes. Within one year you will be married." I was pretty new at listening to the voice of God, but this came with such a gift of faith that I believed it.

The next few months that followed were the most beautiful and intimate months I have ever had with the Lord. Believing that He was going to take care of finding me a spouse allowed me to heal from the past brokenness and delve into the Lord in ways I had never known before. I went to sleep with electric feelings of the Lord's presence and woke up more than five times a night just to say out loud, "I love you Jesus!" Then I would fall back asleep. It continued over and over again night after night after night! My heart was filled with thanksgiving and love for Jesus.

Three months later, while I was cleaning my house, I suddenly thought that maybe I had been wrong about my perception of what the Lord said. I wasn't doubting God; my faith was strong. I was just recognizing that I had been sure in the past that the Lord was telling me certain men would be my husband—and I was wrong. I then realized that most of the times I had been wrong about hearing the Lord it had to do with men. So I told Him that in spite of how sure I was that He would bring my soul mate, I recognized I had a weakness in this area. For two weeks, every day, I prayed that the Lord would reveal the whole thing to someone else. Even though I had not mentioned it to anyone, I prayed that God would use someone to confirm it for me. And He did.

While He Lay Dying

My friend called me up out of the blue and told me that she had had a vision about me. "Lara! I saw him! I saw your husband! I saw you meet him, I saw dates that you went on, I saw you marry him. I know what he looks like!" she said. "I don't normally tell people if I see visions that have to do with marriage, but for some reason the Lord told me that I needed to tell you because you needed to know. It's going to happen soon, Lara! But you need to know something about him...he's tall! Really tall!"

Now being only 5'1" myself, I had set my sights on someone of the short to average variety, and my friend felt she needed to prepare me so that I wouldn't miss the right man simply because I might think he was too tall for me! She wouldn't tell me anything more, but it was all the confirmation I needed. The funny thing is, after this, I stopped looking. I figured the Lord would bring it about it in His time, so I was just going to enjoy life and enjoy Him.

I decided to go on a vacation with Jesus. Why not, right? In March I packed my bags and drove from my hometown of Cranbrook, B.C. to Vancouver to visit with a friend and then caught a flight to Costa Rica where I spent spring break enjoying solitude, sun, and Jesus!

Chapter Two

When I returned from my vacation, I decided to stay with my friend Amy in Abbotsford (near Vancouver) for a few days. I met her friends, and we hung out and prayed together and just had a great time. Amy was finishing up an internship with a ministry there and was ready to come home, so she packed up her life and loaded it into my Subaru.

On March 23rd, 2007, a typical gloomy, rainy West Coast kind of day, she and I set out for Cranbrook, about ten hours' drive away. Just outside the town of Hope (about an hour down the road), my car started to smoke and I no longer had much control. I couldn't shift at all, and then it just sputtered and died. I got out to see what was the matter, but I really didn't have a clue. There I was standing in a downpour beside my crippled car on the side of a mountain road as smoke billowed out of the front end. With no reception on my cell phone, very few dollars in my wallet, and a pressing need to be back at work in a couple of days, I started to bawl. Vehicles sped by, splashing mud my way, but no one would stop.

After about an hour of doing my best damsel in distress impression (which had never failed me before), I gave up hoping anyone would stop and got back into the car to find Amy singing and rejoicing and giving thanks to the Lord! I glared at her.

While He Lay Dying

"I am just so excited to see what God does through this situation!" she chirped.

I knew her attitude was right, but I just couldn't get myself to that place with her. I turned my back to her and her happiness and started to cry again. I knew I needed this car and had just used all my savings to go on my vacation with Jesus.

A couple of hours later, we prayed and turned the ignition key again. This time the car started and had just enough life to coast down the hill into town and to a mechanic's shop, where we learned that the seals were blown, the engine was blown, the clutch was blown—and so were my hopes of going home that day.

So there we were, stuck in "Hope." (I like God's sense of humour.)

Amy managed to call a friend who drove up from Abbotsford and took us back there, apparently just in time for a church service. Amy seemed very pleased, but I was not so sure. The service was about healing; something I had, of course, heard about but not really seen. My faith was weak and my skepticism high, but I was willing to let God change those perceptions. During the service, I became totally enthralled with the love of God, and when the preacher asked people to come to the front for healing, I ran up just to observe. I was watching for "smoke and mirrors," but what I saw was people healed and giving glory to Jesus Christ. I cried as my misperceptions of God and His goodness were beginning to crumble.

In the midst of all of this, I looked over and saw a man standing in the crowd of people, and the Lord clearly said in my heart, "That is your husband."

I dismissed the notion (been there, done that) and went back to watching the people who were being prayed for. I didn't want to miss a single thing. I had never seen anything like this before!

When the service ended, Amy introduced the man I had seen. His name was Bruce, and he was in town for the weekend. I was polite, but I thought little of it. Turns out he didn't think much of meeting me either. He was on his guard with women as he was afraid of being too nice and giving someone the wrong impression (an occupational hazard for handsome, single college professors).

Around midnight a large group of people from the service headed out to Boston Pizza. The restaurant was crowded, and somehow we ended up across from one another at the same table. It was only then I noticed how good looking he was. He had warm sparkly hazel eyes and a perfect smile between charming dimples. I was drawn right away to his strong and masculine facial features, causing a blush to slowly creep up my face. He was obviously athletic, with broad shoulders and a strong build, but it was his wonderful sense of humour that caught me off guard the most.

In a few minutes the noise of the crowd, multiple conversations, and the clinking of dishes and glasses in the room faded away. I was launched into another world with just the two of us as its only inhabitants. He had me in stitches the whole time! I couldn't stop smiling. I can honestly say that to this day I have never had such an exhilarating a conversation as that one. Apparently, it wasn't long before the people around us were watching the two of us talking and laughing. But we never noticed them. We found out later a very prophetic man across the way noticed us and said to the people at his table, "Those two will be married, and they will be pastors."

Later when Amy and I went back into her friend's apartment and were making our beds once more, I was embarrassed to tell even her just how taken I was with this man. I slept with a smile on my face, wondering if I would ever see him again. The next morning I tried to conjure up reasons why we should try to hang out with the same group he was staying with. Meanwhile, he was doing the same. Somehow, we all ended up going for lunch together again, and we spent the rest of the day together.

That evening we were at another church service. I looked over at him, and he looked back at me—and I knew. I just revelled. *So this is what it feels like to meet your husband!* After being in too many relationships where I always felt I was more interested in the other person than he was in me I finally began to have an idea of what it was like to be loved in return. I could see it in his eyes.

I almost forgot about my broken-down car in Hope and the fact that I needed to be back in my classroom ready to teach those energetic first-graders the next day—in a city ten hours' drive away. (I should note that

While He Lay Dying

God loves to restore, and He provided another one of Amy's close friends, who not only drove me back to Cranbrook, but later flew out to Hope from Calgary to put a new engine in my car, for only the cost of parts! (He's an amazing person who just loves to help others.)

A week later, Bruce arranged to come to my hometown to visit Amy and me since he had a week clear of classes at the college where he taught. By the second day of his visit, we were officially dating.

I had agreed to help my friend (the one who had the vision) on a photo shoot a few days later. When she came by the house to pick me up, she met him. I took her aside at the shoot and asked her if he was the one. She refused to tell me—but her eyes twinkled and all day she kept squealing and saying she was so excited for me! Finally, I got it out of her.

"I am 100% positive that he is the exact same person I saw in the vision. He even has the same nose!"

She could also tell me dates we had together and moments she had seen in the vision that no one would have any way of knowing! "Did he visit your school and give piggy-back rides to the kids?" she asked.

I nodded, looking incredulously at her.

"I saw that," she said matter-of-factly.

Two weeks later, Bruce drove to Cranbrook again and this time we went ring shopping.

"Look how sparkly this is," he grinned as he held up a beautiful diamond ring, the sunlight streaming through the jewellery shop window. It was much grander than anything I had ever dreamed of. "Please, let me get this one for you?"

Two weeks after that, he drove the mountain passes again to come and get me so I could meet his family back in his hometown of Kelowna. My parents managed to be in Kelowna that week as well, and they also met Bruce. My dad's response was that I had better marry this guy soon, because he is amazing!

I don't recommend running out and jumping into marriage with someone you have not known very long, however, in this case, the Lord's hand was so evident that we both knew without any doubt that we were meant for each other. Both of our sets of parents agreed.

That same evening, under the shade of a giant spruce tree that Bruce and his father had planted together when he was just a boy and the family was beginning to put down roots in their new country, this wonderful man got down on one knee and asked me, with tears in his gentle eyes, to marry him.

I said yes! Yes, yes, yes!

We planned an autumn wedding beside the turquoise waters of a small lake at the base of the Steeples mountain range near my home four months later. While he was helping to work out the seating arrangement for the reception to follow (by using a graphic diagram on his computer—that's so Bruce), he asked casually if we really needed all these guests.

"You don't realize how drastically she has pared down the list already!" my mom laughed, "Lara really does have that many friends, Bruce. Someday you will be very grateful for her ability to make connections. She has had this gift since she was a child."

My husband was nearing his 33rd birthday and I was 27 when we got married. He had an amazing story of waiting for the right one too. We believe the Lord saved us for each other and that we were meant to be together. We felt His hand, His favour, and His blessings on our union. In fact, after our outdoor wedding, when we walked back up the "aisle" together, we stepped straight into double rainbows stretched down low under the snow-tipped mountains like a canopy of promise.

At the airport upon returning from our honeymoon in Spain, my mother met us and declared, "Happy Thanksgiving, you two!"

Ah! Thanksgiving! One year—exactly. Thank You, Jesus!

God doesn't always speak so clearly and loudly to me as He did in this situation. I tend to think He only speaks loudly in times when He really needs to, for whatever reason. I know at that point I needed it because I had been hurt, and I wouldn't have been able or willing to give my heart to another without so clear a leading.

Chapter Three

Exactly a year after we met, we sat down in the office of one of the leading gynecologists in the Lower Mainland area. I had known for a number of years that I had a serious case of endometriosis, a disease in which the tissue lining the uterus grows outside the confines of the womb and expands, attaching itself to other internal organs. I had been told that as a result of the effects of this disease, it was likely that I would not be able to conceive my own children. This doctor not only confirmed the information I had been given but also told us that the prognosis was far worse than he had first thought. Upon surgical exploration of my abdomen, he discovered that my right ovary (which had been reconstructed in a previous related surgery) would not function properly. I had anticipated that, but what I hadn't anticipated was that he found the left side was deformed and also unlikely able to work, and to top it off both fallopian tubes were completely blocked!

I went home downcast, because all I had ever dreamed of being was a mother. I even became a teacher because I thought it was the best training I could think of for motherhood. Full of faith, Bruce looked at me and said, "The bigger the problem, the bigger the miracle!"

He knew we would have children. He just knew it. Despite attacks that he had felt on his own fertility, he always knew that God was going to prevail in this promise to him and that we would bear children.

Many things about Bruce amaze me. One of my favourite things is his faith. He has faith for the impossible. In fact, the more impossible the situation looks, the more excited Bruce seems to get. He has a way of changing my perspective to focus not on how big the problem is but rather how much bigger God is than the problem.

The gynecologist said he would try to force a little dye through the fallopian tubes, but he was sure they would immediately clog up again. He recommended a treatment that put me into temporary menopause. He hoped it would slow down the progress of the disease and give me relief from the pain for a while. Perhaps later I could try fertility drugs.

A couple months later, unexpectedly, five different people—mostly strangers from other parts of the world—came up to me and all said the same thing. They said the Lord told them to tell me that I was going to have a baby. With the first few, I just stared at them and said thank you. By the time the last couple of people repeated the same message, my faith caught up and I began to feel an excitement that I would be healed!

When I saw the gynecologist again for a follow-up appointment, he gave me a prescription for fertility drugs, saying that since he was able to open my tubes a bit by forcing dye through, this might be my only chance of conceiving—if I used the drugs. Now, I actually don't have any problem with God using modern medicine as a solution, but in talking with Bruce, we both wanted to give God a chance to get the glory in this. So with the measure of faith we had, we decided to leave the prescription slip in my wallet for one month and not get it filled. Turns out I never had to take the pills—within a month we were pregnant with our first child!

The doctor's office was baffled! I expected God to do it, but in only one month? Wow! Words can't even describe the joy and love we were feeling. It felt so right, so normal, and yet so extraordinary! Our families were shocked and so excited! This would be Bruce's parents' first grandchild. They had already resigned themselves to probably never having any. Can you imagine the joy and celebrations that went on when we told them?

We had a miracle conception, but to be honest, the pregnancy was difficult with severe nausea and vomiting that lasted nearly the whole 40 weeks and ten days. Our daughter was born in the wee hours of March 24, exactly two years after we met in the wee hours of the night at the table in Boston Pizza and exactly one year after the fertility specialist told us a natural pregnancy would probably never happen. (That day was also Bruce's mother's birthday.) We named our miracle child Keziah Joy (pronounced KEZ-ee-ah) after one of Job's daughters, given to him after the Lord restored everything to him. Her name is a constant reminder to us that our God is a God who redeems even the worst circumstances.

Shortly before her birth, we had moved to Lethbridge, Alberta. When she was about nine months old, another gynecologist, who suspected the endometriosis was getting worse, advised us to not delay trying to conceive again as he thought the odds of us having another child were not very good. Once more, we conceived without any trouble—again, within one month! Just 16 months after our daughter was born, I gave birth to our son, Axel Veritas, the following summer. His name means "father of peace and truth."

When Axel was a few months old, I had another laparoscopy to deal with the endometriosis. I typically had this done every two years to scrape the extra endometrial tissue growth off my internal organs. I had a new doctor, who was not familiar with how severe the disease had been in the past. He called me at home after the procedure and told me I had a very minor case and that all my organs were completely normal! I kept asking him if he was sure nothing was deformed or clogged. "Are you sure?" I asked him, "Are you sure nothing is deformed or clogged?"

"Yes, Lara. Everything appears to be normal in there," he assured.

He must have thought I was a hypochondriac the way I had been going on about how serious it was. After all, only six years earlier I had nearly died after hemorrhaging when an orange-sized "chocolate cyst" had ruptured, suddenly and painfully, bleeding into my abdomen. I was teaching in a private school on a small Caribbean island at the time and required immediate emergency surgery in a tiny third-world hospital there. God provided an excellent gynecologist who got me into surgery immediately, but she was the one who first broke the news that I could expect a life of chronic pain and infertility problems.

Two years later, on January 2nd, 2013, we welcomed our *third* child. Once again we had had no difficulty getting pregnant on the first try! It's amazing that every miracle baby is just as exciting to us as the last. I knew with the coming of this child that there would be a season of change. We felt the Lord gave us the name Vivia Charity, "full of life and love." When our pastor and bishop, Todd Atkinson, came to the hospital to meet her, he said the Latin word "viva" was also the root word for revival. That fit just right. "Revival of love." Little did I know what we would soon be walking through to see such a revival come to life.

Chapter Four

You need to know that we are a really normal family. Our days are filled with diapers, squabbles, skinned knees, misunderstandings, simple joys, interrupted sleep, and hard work like most people. If you met us, I imagine you would quickly learn we are very similar to other people you might know.

Both Bruce and I are teachers by trade, and we currently teach hundreds of students online and love it. We drive a minivan, gain weight and lose weight (at least a few times a year), watch football and hockey, and live a pretty regular Canadian life.

You may be wondering what background we come from. I grew up in a missions-minded evangelical church and attended conservative evangelical churches in university. Just before I met Bruce, I felt the Lord urging me to step out of my comfort zone and into charismatic circles, which is where Bruce mostly grew up. I've been conservative evangelical as well as charismatic, and I have had the pleasure of seeing the beauty of God working in both. I have a deep love for all of the brothers and sisters in Christ and in the Church across the world. We currently attend a "convergent" church that embraces and celebrates evangelical, charismatic, and historical theology and practices all at the same time—a three-stream church, so to speak.

While He Lay Dying

We first moved to Lethbridge, Alberta, just before the birth of our first child so that Bruce could take a pastoral position at River of Life Community Church under the mentorship of the lead pastor, and now Bishop, Todd Atkinson. Bruce left his comfort zone of being an amazing math teacher and began using his gifts and talents in the church, first assisting a dear long-time friend, Pastor Jep Banda, in the children's program, and then moving on to lead in the areas of missions, prayer, and internship supervision.

Bruce's heart yearned to see the church awaken to the riches of personal prayer and the power of corporate prayer. At one point he set up a board in the foyer with time slots that covered every hour of every day 24/7. He encouraged people to write their name in a slot on a chart to pray during that time every week. The board may have been 50 percent filled in, with perhaps about 30 percent of the church participating. When he held teaching sessions on prayer and how to hear the voice of God, a good number of people in our church attended, though he had hoped it would catch on even more. He laboured to try and teach people how to pray corporately and to listen and move together with whatever the Holy Spirit was doing.

Bruce has always been a striver. When something weighs on his heart, he does everything he can to make it happen. He longs for excellence. He approaches everything with an attitude of a skilled German engineer posing the question: "How can we perform this task faster, more efficiently, and to the highest quality?" In fairness, this trait has often served him well. He has accomplished four degrees—two of them Masters degrees. He has won scholarships, awards, and accolades in academics and the teaching profession. He thinks fast, talks fast, moves fast, yet is kind, down to earth, and considerate of everyone whether or not they can keep up to him. Both kids and adults love him. His bearing commands authority when he walks into a classroom or a meeting, but his gentle manner and kind voice put people at ease. He has a natural talent for music and athletics. For some reason I have never really tried as hard to excel as much as he has, but I have noticed that sometimes it is actually harder for someone who has always had the ability to do things easily to depend on God and wait for Him to do it His way.

After a couple of years of working at River of Life, the Lord clearly led us to take the valuable lessons we had learned while pastoring back into the field of education. We both work for an amazing Christian online school. Bruce began by developing an advanced placement calculus course for them and moved into writing more courses and teaching mathematics online. After earning my education degree and teaching kindergarten and grade one for a few years, I apprenticed with a popular photographer and then started my own business. I combined those skills to develop and teach an online photography course as well. It is exciting to see the potential this method of teaching has for North American homeschoolers as well as for children of families overseas and students in third-world countries without easy access to quality education. I love that the Lord can lead us out of traditional ministry in a way that is healthy while still keeping intact our love for our church, its people, and our dear friends. I love that the Lord can lead us to minister in a completely different way. Although Bruce was no longer using a traditional ministry platform, he was still pastoring and mentoring, only this time to students. The job title had changed, but the heart and the call to ministry burned just as brightly.

We hadn't left our church but were still very involved there. Bruce, being Bruce, never really took off his caring pastoral hat. He continued to meet with people, to listen, to pray with them, to encourage them, and to build them up in faith to be Christ's people in their own spheres of influence and calling.

Over the next couple of years, the church began moving increasingly toward a lifestyle of prayer. We began meeting once a month, then twice a month for all-night prayer vigils. A sense of anticipation that God was about to do something among us grew and excited people about praying together, even praying all night.

As it turned out, the prayer vigils were a necessary training ground for what was about to follow.

Chapter Five

Day 1—Saturday (March 23, 2013)

Late in March of 2013 as I was beginning to prepare for Keziah's fourth birthday party that coming Saturday morning, Bruce looked at me with that look men get when they are under the weather. He said he had the flu and that it hit him like a wall. He then went and laid down—for three days. I was quite frustrated with him, frankly. This was not good timing!

I blame my brother, my dad, and Bruce and every other man I have met for introducing me to the "man cold." I remember the story of my brother dragging his poor sore-throat-stuffy-head-cough-ridden body into the drug store and asking the pharmacist for the most effective medication.

She started clapping her hands over her head and said with a raised voice, "Attention! Attention everybody! There is a man here with a cold!"

You can get away with that in a small town, and I understood her. She was probably a mother who never had the luxury of lying in bed for three days when she felt sick—especially if her child was all excited and expecting a birthday party. All of Keziah's friends were coming, with their parents, not to mention both sets of grandparents!

While He Lay Dying

By this point I could tell my husband was legitimately sick, but I was still recovering from my third C-section and getting up at night with a new baby, chasing a toddler, and keeping an exceptionally curious, industrious, almost-four-year-old occupied, and now I had to do everything for this party—by myself.

Over the next couple days, the tension mounted as I cleaned and prepared rooms for the grandparents coming from out of town and started to decorate and prepare food for the party. Thanks to my sleep-deprived memory, I had dressed the kids in their winter hats, mitts, coats, and boots, herded or carried them out to the mini-van and strapped them into their car seats for more trips to the store and back for things I had forgotten than I care to admit. Every once in a while I ran downstairs to the spare room (I had evicted Bruce from our room so the baby and I wouldn't get sick too and so he could sleep undisturbed) to make sure he was okay.

He didn't look well. The thermometer read 39.7 Celsius (103.5 Fahrenheit), and he started complaining of pain in his left hamstring that felt like a pulled muscle. That seemed odd since he hadn't done anything recently that might have caused such an injury. I asked him if he could have an infection, and we checked his leg. It wasn't red or swollen, and there were no cuts, so we considered it an unfortunate coincidence. I gave him some Ibuprofen and Tylenol and went back to the mounds of work I needed to do, grumbling under my breath about the timing of this.

On Friday, the day when our parents were due to arrive from B.C., he seemed no better. In fact, he seemed worse. He had his phone on alarm so he would know exactly when he could take the next dose of meds—and this from a man who rarely ever took painkillers. Our parents showed up that evening, and he dragged himself out to the kitchen to say hello, but he was limping heavily and didn't have the strength to sit and visit, so he went back to bed, upstairs in our room this time.

That night he never slept a wink. He was rolling around and writhing in pain. I was confused. I had never seen a pulled muscle cause that much pain before. Was he over-reacting or was it something else? What could it be, though? I suggested he should go to the hospital, but he wanted to be there for his little girl's birthday. In the morning, half an hour before our house was due to be filled with kids and their parents, he finally agreed to go to the emergency room in hopes that at least they could give him some more powerful drugs than what we had at home to stop the pain.

"Dad, could you drive him?" I asked my father.

"I'll get my keys," he said.

They decided to drive to a hospital in a small town close by so they could get right in to see a doctor. Bruce hated the thought of sitting in a crowded waiting room with that much pain from what he was sure would be considered a minor, non-critical hamstring injury. He was seen immediately at the small hospital, and when they took his blood pressure it was found to be very low. They also gave him intravenous fluids for dehydration. He told them he hadn't peed in 24 hours. They suspected that his kidneys were possibly failing, and the ER doctor conferred with doctors in Lethbridge who recommended he be sent back to the city to be admitted for an immediate ultrasound. On the way, in the ambulance, his blood pressure dipped even lower.

My father called to let us know what was happening. This is right about the time the party was wrapping up. Our friends were disappointed to have missed Bruce and were concerned for him. A couple of them stayed to help clean up and wait for news. I was able to drive over to the hospital to meet Bruce when he arrived. When I saw him, he was still writhing in pain. He said that on a scale of one to ten, he rated his pain a twelve, despite all the morphine and fentanyl he had been given. It was then that I learned that his kidneys were failing. I sat beside him, inside the cubicle created by the pastel yellow and turquoise plaid curtain drawn around his bed, and watched the numbers on the machine that recorded his blood pressure drop even lower.

The internal medicine specialist came in after about an hour and said that they had found a pocket of fluid in his left hamstring and that's what was causing the pain. He said it was indicative of an infection, so they were going to move him up to the ICU. Now.

I hadn't had a lot of experience with hospitals, so I didn't really get what was going on or what they thought might happen. I knew ICUs were for really sick people though. Why were they sending Bruce there if he only needed antibiotics? At that point, I left the ER to call our family at home and to let our pastor, Bishop Todd Atkinson, know what was going on. I also texted our friend Dr. Stephen Crawford, who worked at the hospital. Dr. Crawford was Bruce's doctor when we first moved to Lethbridge. They remained good friends after Steve left his office practice and took on the position of lead hospitalist. He had supported me over the phone the year before when Bruce's appendix had ruptured while we were on a work trip in South Africa and was an amazing help when it came to translating medical terms. He was reassuring about what was going on.

The transfer took a while. In the ICU, the nurses added more IV's and finally got his pain under control. Then they let me in to see him. Bishop Todd came shortly after, and Bruce was his normal joking self, making the nurses laugh. He had Todd and I in stitches!

"We're making arrangements to take you into the OR to see if we can find out what is happening in this leg of yours," the specialist said when he came in.

"This will probably be just a quick surgery and you'll be out of here in a couple of days," I said to my husband. I really thought that's all it would be.

The surgery lasted two hours, and since he was still sedated, Bruce looked peaceful when he came out of the recovery room. The doctor told me they found necrotizing fasciitis (flesh-eating disease) in his leg and that the surgeon had cut his leg open from behind his knee on the back of his left leg up to his bottom. He said they were going to leave it open for a while to let it seep and to make sure that all the infection was gone.

At this point, the text messages from concerned friends were coming in like mad. Many people had heard Bruce was in hospital, so in an effort to write things only once I posted this on Facebook:

Update for those praying for Bruce Merz. He just came out of emergency surgery. They found Flesh Eating Disease from his bottom to his knee on his left leg. And he has been cut all the way down and they've left it open to drain. His kidneys are doing very poorly, but because he is young and healthy, they should come back to health in three or four days. He is in ICU and will likely be hospitalized for at least two weeks.

Dr. said it will be a long painful recovery. Please pray that he will recover quickly and with very little pain, and no problems with his leg hereafter! Thank you all who have been praying and passing word around. We have felt your prayers! We can't even express how thankful we are that they caught this in time. He was saved from something horrible and possibly fatal! Thank you all so much for the well wishes and prayers!! We feel so loved!!

This is when the tears started to flow. Flesh eating disease? What is that?! People can die from that, right?!!

I called Dr. Crawford immediately to try to grasp what was really going on. With my permission, he looked up Bruce's file and told me that it looked like they got it early and they got all the infection out, so he should make a good recovery. He wasn't worried about death, nor was the specialist. It looked like they got it in time and Bruce would recover and get better. However, they said they would likely keep him asleep for a few days while the wound was open and then he would just need to rest and recuperate.

Standing in Bruce's room at 10:00 pm that night, I looked at the nurse and I realized I didn't know what to do. What do people do when their spouse is sick? Should I sit by his side all night? Will it help him? Will it help me? What about my two-month-old baby at home who can't come into the ICU? What do I do with her?

"What should I do?" I asked the nurse as she checked the IV tubes. "I mean, what do people do in a situation like this? I have a new baby at home who needs me, and I want to be with my husband, but he's sleeping and I don't know how to help him."

She saw the tears in my eyes.

"Go home, dear. He's stable and resting. You need sleep, and your baby needs you. Bruce won't even know you're here. Just go home and come back in the morning."

So I went home feeling like I was leaving half of me there but trusting the Lord that I was doing the right thing.

Chapter Six

Day 2—Sunday

My sleep was fitful at best, and I held my phone in my hands all night just in case it rang. When I got up early the next morning with the baby, the first thing I did was call the ICU. I expected them to tell me everything was okay, that he was the same as before and he was getting better, but that is not the message I got.

The nurse told me that they had struggled to keep Bruce alive all night. Apparently his blood pressure plummeted rapidly even on the meds. They had added another medication and upped them both to nearly the highest doses they can give, and he just hung on with a minimal blood pressure. I was told that he nearly flatlined twice that night because he had no blood pressure on his own. His body was going into full septic shock. His kidneys were getting worse. His blood was poisoned, and because the blood flows everywhere through the body, his whole system had begun to shut down.

After making a very brief post on Facebook asking people to pray, I ran to the car and drove furiously to the hospital not knowing what I would find or what I should expect. They had kept him on the ventilator ever since the surgery (apparently they knew how this type of thing can go), and he was deeply sedated. Outside his room stood a whole group of different specialists (surgeons, internal medicine specialists, a kidney specialist, a blood specialist, and at least two nurses) all discussing his case. I don't know that in my life and experience that I have ever seen someone I know and love need more than one specialist at a time!

It was Sunday morning at about 10:00 am, half an hour before the second service, when I texted Bishop Todd to tell him what was happening. He had already seen my Facebook post from that morning. On Palm Sunday morning, in a large church full of expectant people waiting for a sermon and just before he was about to speak, our pastor walked away from the pulpit, handing the microphone off to an assistant pastor. Love was louder than words as Todd rushed to the hospital. I have seen dedicated pastors, but I'd never seen this! Not only did he come to Bruce's side straightaway, but he also stayed in Bruce's room for the following 23 hours straight.

One of the other pastors stepped in at the church, and a couple more pastors and dear friends showed up at the hospital while the church service was going on to hug me and pray with me. I felt so loved! I've always known my own love for my husband, but I began to have a glimpse of the depth to which others loved him too as we cried together.

That day was our daughter's official birthday, as well as Bruce's mother's 70th birthday. It was also exactly six years from the day that we sat facing each other in Boston Pizza and five years from the day we were told we would likely never have children. Here is the Facebook post that came from that:

> Today my beautiful eldest daughter turns four. We named her Keziah after Job's daughter to always remind us that our God is a God who redeems even the worst circumstances. She was a miracle through and through, and I am thankful for the unique, spunky, bold, sensitive, and intelligent person that she is! She truly is a reminder of God's goodness and his ability to move in the miraculous. I think I need that reminder today.
>
> As I laid awake alone in bed last night, I remembered that this weekend marks exactly six years from the day Bruce and I laid eyes on each other for the first time. Sometimes I think Kezi was my first miracle but

it's not true; Bruce was my first miracle. I knew from the first moment I first talked to him that he was going to be my husband. He has been my husband, my best friend, and my soul mate, and the Lord never ceases to bless me with that man. I'm proud to stand by his side as we walk through this together with God! Thanks all for your love. I cry just about every time I read how many are praying for us. Please pray that Kezi's birthday will still be special for her!

Facebook was only really intended at first as a vehicle to get the information out to those friends and family that kept texting me and wanted to be kept in the loop. It soon became something so much bigger than I ever imagined. Friends started re-posting my posts, inviting others to pray for Bruce. I had no idea how many people were going to read them.

Later that morning they took Bruce to get a CT scan to see if the infection had grown, which would explain why his body was going into such severe shock. The scan came back negative, and for the time being it seemed like they had gotten everything and all we had to worry about was Bruce recovering from the severe septic shock. At one point that afternoon, Bruce opened his eyes. He couldn't talk because he had a tube down his throat, but he was desperately trying to communicate. We tried holding a pad of paper for him, but he just wrote words on top of each other. I told him Todd was there, and he wanted me to get him. Then he asked for his good friend Jerry too. For about 45 minutes, the boys laughed their heads off as they figured out a system for Bruce to communicate with them. Jerry went through the alphabet and Bruce gave thumbs up or down to each letter and Todd transcribed:

"I have pretty nice handwriting for a circus midget, don't I?" he "wrote."

It made no sense to me, but it really got Jerry and Todd laughing. (I think it may have been an inside joke. Bruce was used to often being the tallest person in a room—especially around my family—but Todd is even taller.) It was just enough of a glimpse of Bruce and his humour to make us feel like he was in there and he was happy.

The nurse kicked everyone out because she was concerned Bruce was getting too worked up. He was completely out again within minutes of them leaving. She told me later she didn't understand how

Bruce could have woken up. When she had taken him down to the CT scan, they had to move him all over the place, which should have been excruciating for him, and he didn't even flinch. She said he was very deeply sedated. Then he woke up, was totally with it, cracking jokes and making everyone laugh (even though his jokes made no sense). And then moments later he was out cold again, just as deeply sedated as before. I told her it was the Lord blessing us, so that we could know that Bruce was still with us.

Later that evening I sat at the hospital searching my heart for what would bring the peace I needed and I was reminded of Philippians 4:4-9:

> "Rejoice in the Lord always. I will say it again: Rejoice! Let your gentleness be evident to all. The Lord is near. Do not be anxious about anything, but in every situation, by prayer and petition, *with thanksgiving*, present your requests to God. And the peace of God, which transcends all understanding, will guard your hearts and your minds in Christ Jesus." (Emphasis added.)

When my friend (our worship pastor) Dave asked me if there was anything he could do for me, I told him we needed to worship and asked if he would host a worship night at his place that night. At the same time, there were at least two separate prayer meetings for Bruce happening at people's homes. I later found out that many other people in groups and churches around the world were also meeting to pray for Bruce. Word of his condition was spreading rapidly via social media. I had no idea how rapidly.

On my way to Dave's house, I received a phone call from a previous pastor of Bruce's back in Kelowna whom I had never met. He called to tell me that he and his wife had been on their knees praying for Bruce and that he had felt strongly that this was an attack from the enemy on Bruce's life and his calling.[2] This was actually the second time I had heard the same thing that day, and my spirit agreed.

We were in a war with the enemy, and so I did what I know the enemy hates. I sang! I rejoiced! And I gave thanks! I was filled and overwhelmed

---

[2] "The thief comes only to steal and kill and destroy; I have come that they may have life, and have it to the full" (John 10:10, Jesus speaking).

with love: God's love for Bruce, God's love for me, the love of our congregation, and just the sheer number of people who loved my husband!

While I was singing at Dave's house, I saw a vision. It was a vision of Jesus by Bruce's bedside with His head resting on Bruce's arm. There was so much tangible love in the hospital room, and then it started to fill with angels! Angels packed the room like a clown car. Every square inch was filled with angels. So much love, so much peace.

In the meantime, an old college roommate of mine started an event page on Facebook to gather people to pray and keep them updated on Bruce's condition. Over the next few days, over a thousand people joined up. My Facebook posts were being re-posted there as well.

I went back to the hospital that night in peace to hold my husband's cold hand and dream of our future together. I found that whenever I spoke about Bruce, I didn't want to call him my husband, like it didn't convey enough of what he meant to me. I just wanted to use the words *soul mate* every time instead of his name, because I knew that God had brought us dramatically together and that he was the one for me. He wasn't replaceable in my mind.

Most of the medical staff were telling me, "You have a very sick husband," but I didn't know what that meant. What does "very" mean? I would say my kids are very sick if they're throwing up. But what does it mean when a person in the *ICU* is very sick? Is that their kind way of saying they think he's going to die? Are they just giving me hope, or do they think he'll get better?

Nurses in the ICU usually sit at a desk just outside the glass wall of a critically ill patient's room. At first, I couldn't see Bruce's nurse when I walked toward the room, but that was because he had moved all his paperwork *into* the room so he could be right beside him.

"I have rarely ever had to stay this close to a patient," he said, never taking his eyes off the machine that flashed numbers giving information about vitals. "But what is happening is that Bruce is so dependent on the medication for his blood pressure, that if there's any interruption at all in the drip, he goes downhill fast and could flatline in less than a minute."

Sometimes, if the meds ran out or if there was a bubble in the line, one of the machines would sound an alarm and shut off until the problem was fixed or the IV bag of meds was changed. In Bruce's case when this happened, I could literally watch his blood pressure drop from 90 to 80 to 70 to 60 to 50 to 40 in a matter of seconds. I often saw the nurses running to get it going again or frantically tap the IV line with a pen to get the bubble out so his heart wouldn't stop. One of the men who was at his bedside night after night told me later the friends who were in there praying for him were trained to throw themselves against a wall as soon as there was a "beep" on any of the machines, because inevitably a nurse would come running into the room. The ICU eventually set up backups for the machines, and even backups for the backups, to try to prevent any potentially fatal interruptions.

As the night wore on, the hospital waiting room filled with friends and former colleagues who loved Bruce. A team of five or six stayed all night and prayed by his bedside. Bruce's brother Mark and his cousin David flew in from Kelowna that night to join them.

At about 2:00 am, I went home to be with our baby. My mother was sitting up with her rocking her in the swing. Vivia's tummy was often upset due to reflux, and she didn't want to take a bottle. She had a hard time settling. She woke up when I came in, and I took her to bed with me. My tears dripped on her head as I held her close and prayed that she would know her daddy. I think her sweet warmth comforted me as much as I comforted her.

When she finally fell asleep, I laid her in her bassinet beside my bed, but now I couldn't sleep. Sleep seemed to elude me. It is easy to go through a kind of denial when you are busy and there are other people around, but when you are lying in bed alone staring at the spot where your husband should be, there is no denying that he is not there. I wept and wept through the nights, because not having him with me was horrible. I had never been through anything this traumatic before. Any other time we faced difficulties, Bruce would be there talking me through it, giving me a heavenly perspective and encouraging my faith. As the closest person in my life, I needed to talk to him!

Chapter Seven

Day 3—Monday

Day 3 was a day that I would have preferred to spend sitting in the waiting room instead of Bruce's room. They had to fill him up with IV fluids; however, because of the kidney failure he couldn't urinate, and so he gained weight at a rapid pace. In the first three days, he gained 78 pounds, swelling him up to over 300 pounds! Bruce is a tall muscular man with a large frame to begin with, but now he looked like the *Hulk*! He was *huge*! His weight eventually topped out at 330 pounds! His forearms were like Popeye's. His shoulders were so massive they almost took over his neck, and his face was distorted and unfamiliar. When I looked at him, I felt like this must be somebody else's husband because mine doesn't look like that guy! There was very little that was recognizable about him.

The medications directed blood to his vital organs, and doing that meant the limbs and extremities would lose the circulation they needed. So here is this *massive* man with cold, pale, and stiff discoloured legs and arms. When I held his hand, it felt like the hand of a corpse. I won't lie; his body felt dead to the touch. I didn't want to touch him. I didn't want to see him like that. I stood in the room for 10 minutes at a time, watching the monitor track his racing heart as it reached 150 beats per minute, and then found refuge in the waiting room full of our friends and family.

The main corridor ran from the elevators, past the delivery unit, past the OR on one side and the Intensive Care Unit on the other, down to the doctors' and nurses' lounges at the end of the hall. Many of Bruce's friends often paced that corridor late at night, praying. When they needed a break, they would push through a set of big heavy doors into a short hallway connecting to the ICU, and turn into the small ICU waiting room, where I spent a lot of my time. Though the room had chipped salmon-coloured walls and worn mismatched chairs from the nineties, it had been transformed from a cold, lonely, isolated area to a place filled 24 hours a day with people praying, singing softly, or sipping coffee—and most importantly, laughing. I cannot even express how amazing laughter is in a time like this. It might seem foreign or unloving to people reading this, but you must remember that the Lord was carrying me and our family through this time. The atmosphere in that place held such peace and joy that a nurse asked one of my friends, "Do you think Lara realizes how serious this situation is?"

Yes, I realized, and at times I almost despaired, especially alone at night, but I also had a sense of love, joy, and peace that could only come from a supernatural download from God. To observers, the circumstances certainly didn't warrant it.

We have a few friends who can't help but be funny all the time, and they were a Godsend to me. I needed the emotional break and the ability to experience the joy of the Lord despite how grave the circumstances looked. The waiting room became a safe place for me. It was a place where I could experience any and all emotions, a place where I was loved relentlessly, and a place of praise and prayer. Bruce's parents, his brother, and my family all felt the same. People were constantly stocking the room with food and water for everyone who was there. It became an oasis of hope.

I realized a lot about myself in those moments. In all honesty, I have never known how to act around people who were experiencing tragedy or loss or sickness. I never knew what to do. I was scared of offending, of saying something wrong. I figured that everyone wanted to be left alone to cry without someone watching. So I did nothing.

Yup, nothing. No baking, no hugs, nothing—at least nothing they could see, anyway. I prayed and wept for them, but I never approached them. Now I know that people who are walking these dark roads need everything—literally everything. They may not even realize it but they need to be pursued; they need to be loved relentlessly in the crisis and for a long time afterward as well.

Right from the start people were asking me what they could do to help, and I would politely say, "Oh, nothing. Just pray—please pray!" It only took a day or two to realize there was absolutely no way I could find time to even go to the store. I had no idea how to feed my children or the up to fifteen people who were camped out at my house. I couldn't even keep food down, let alone think of meal planning. Everyone else at the house was either a family member or a close friend of Bruce, and they were also too distracted to think about shopping and cooking for a crowd every day. About the tenth time someone asked how they could help, I finally squeaked out, "I don't know how to feed everyone..." That very day a friend set up a volunteer meal schedule, and for the next two months the doorbell rang around 5:30 pm and someone would be standing at the door with a fully cooked dinner—a yummy one too!—with enough food for everyone and leftovers galore.

The truth is, there were tons of things I needed help with, and as soon as I got over my pride and was able to ask freely without shame, there was always a line-up of people ready to help take on a task. The other truth is that they needed to help as much as I needed to admit I needed help. In fact, one beautiful aspect was that many people started to see how the natural talents or skills or resources they already had could be put to use to help us. Our church responded in ways that blew my mind; not only was food covered, but someone with a lawn-care company did my yard work, a hot tub company took care of sterilizing and testing the hot tub, handymen fixed things around the house. People helped with childcare and cleaned the van. Groups of women came to clean my house or randomly showed up at the door with gifts for the kids, toilet paper, toothpaste, and Starbucks drinks. At the same time, some of my dearest friends even drove up from British Columbia to fold laundry, take care of my children, and just love on me.

While He Lay Dying

When one girl showed up at my door with a large box filled with necessities and treats for us, I felt so humbled. Her sister had gone missing the year before and was later declared the victim of murder. What had I done in her crisis? Nothing. I didn't want to be nosy or be a bother so I did nothing. But there she was at my door, saying she knew what it was like to be in crisis and she wanted to help meet my needs. Wow. How often do we let pride or embarrassment get in the way of true community? We were designed for community. We were never meant to carry every load alone.

I wonder if by reading this some of you may be reminded of times when you were in crisis and are saying to yourself, "Where was everybody? No one was coming to my door. Nobody seemed to care." I'm sorry if this brings up painful memories. I recognize there are many dynamics, and each person's story is different. I simply want to tell you about a community that responded with tremendous love. And that response did not come by chance. Before our family's ordeal, our church family had been working hard at becoming a loving community. Bruce gave time and attention to many people who needed an understanding listener and encouragement, so for them coming to our rescue was a natural expression of their love and relationship to him. He also had good friends there in whom he could confide. They in turn listened and encouraged him and were instantly at his hospital bedside when he needed them.

Every meaningful relationship requires give and take. Many of us have been taught not to expose our brokenness or our weakness, because people might think we are seeking sympathy and not taking responsibility for our own problems. We were taught that vulnerability is weakness and that being strong means bearing our own pain privately and not bothering others with it. True, it is not easy to take the risk of being transparent, but how else will people know we need help? On the other hand, some of us absorbed the message early in life that we are not as competent as others and that more often than not we will probably be on the receiving end of help rather than on the giving end. Stepping up to support other people when we lack confidence can feel like taking a risk as well, but this is how we grow together. Community requires trust.

Not every church is a good fit for every person; some people feel more comfortable in different settings, but the search is worth it. Community takes a lot of time, a lot of investment, a lot of forgiveness, a lot of personal healing, and a lot of patience. I just want to share our experience with a church that endeavours to be a safe, loving, supportive place.

The surprising thing was how, over and over again, I heard people thanking me for inviting them into my crisis! I didn't understand at first what they meant because I was mostly acting out of my desperate need to be surrounded by people who would pray for Bruce. I am an extravert by nature, and I try to live a transparent life, so inviting people to come and cry with me came relatively easily. I began to understand however, as people I didn't know that well filled the seats in the waiting room in the wee hours and throughout the day, that they also wanted to feel part of this somehow. They needed to know they weren't in the way and that I wanted them there. I know that for some personalities, inviting others to join them in their pain and crisis is not easy. I'm not sure that they have to; we all grieve and function differently and God made us all so uniquely it would be a shame for me to tell you how you should or shouldn't respond. But I will say this, if you don't invite people in, you will likely be alone. There were times I didn't want hugs and times I wanted to be alone, so I told people that and they always respected me. But that room full of people was my place of peace.

> "Two are better than one, because they have a good return for their labor: If either of them falls down, one can help the other up. But pity anyone who falls and has no one to help them up...A cord of three strands is not quickly broken" (Ecclesiastes 4:9-10,12b).

Eventually I realized that I couldn't be there all the time. I was a mother of three very young children. Every time I left Bruce, I felt like I left half of me at the hospital. It felt wrong to leave him, like my being there would somehow make all the difference, but every time I was at the hospital, I felt like I should be at home with my children, making life feel as normal as possible, playing and laughing so they wouldn't have to be worried about Daddy. No matter where I was, I didn't feel like I was in the right place. Sleeping, eating, and showering just seemed like a waste of precious time that could be spent with the kids or with Bruce. (Don't worry. I couldn't keep that lifestyle up for long, and I eventually started showering and sleeping again. Eating came last, but it came when my stomach was ready to handle it.)

Fortunately, we were so unbelievably blessed to have had both sets of grandparents visiting when this all happened. Our kids love their amazing grandparents, and they helped to make life feel normal. My kids never knew the severity of what was going on. At two months, two-and-a-half years, and barely four years old, I didn't think it would be good for them to know that Daddy could die.

I recalled a conversation Keziah and I had shared not long after baby Vivia was born. A warm chinook wind had peeled back the blanket of snow in the park, and we were able to get outside for a little stroll. As we walked past an old flower bed, she looked up at me and said, "We don't know what it feels like to be dead. That's a'cause we've never been dead before so we don't know how it feels." She looked at me for agreement.

I nodded.

She went on, "And if you're dead, then you're dead and you can't tell anyone a'cause you're dead." She paused and thought about it for a few minutes, while shuffling her heavy winter boots down the sidewalk. "But maybe we could ask the flowers a'cause they die every winter so they know how it feels…Too bad they don't have mouths, or they would prolly tell us!"

I remember thinking at the time, *What three year old thinks about death?* And now I wondered, *What three-year-old thinks about being raised from something that* looks *like death?*

On a short break at home, I held the oldest two on my lap and told them, "Daddy is really sick, and he has a really big owie on his leg. He is going to be away for a while in the hospital."

"Does it hurt him a lot?" Kezi asked.

"Not right now, honey, because he is still sleeping."

"I have a owie too, Mommy," Axel said, searching for a freckle-sized scratch on his leg. He went off limping the way Bruce limped the last time he saw him. "I need a Band-Aid."

"Of course you do, Sweetie," and I went and got him one.

They really did need me though. More than they have ever needed me before, they needed me now. We could have a house filled with helpful people, but only Mommy could change a diaper right or put the lid on a sippy cup right or cut the crusts off a piece of bread right. Most of the time, they were happy with all the attention from grandparents, cousins and uncles and aunts and Mommy's friends, but sometimes they unexpectedly expressed explosive emotions over simple things. I saw my sweet kind children raging in their rooms and trashing everything they could find. My heart broke for them, and yet I had to do my best to maintain consistent discipline for their safety and everyone else's. After a while, my son stopped eating. All of these things would war in my heart; I needed to be there for them, but I needed to be at the hospital with Bruce too.

While I was at home with my son that same day, he jabbered on about this and that, laughing and playing. Then he stopped. He looked at me very seriously and said, "We don't hass to be afraid, Mommy. We don't hass to be afraid because Jesus is wis us! Jesus is wis us, Mommy, Jesus is wis us!!" and then he went back to talking about his toys. Oh, how I love it when the Lord speaks to me through my children!

And every day more people were praying. We heard from missionaries and pastors who led churches around the world that were praying. A friend in another city posted a prayer request on his Facebook page, and someone left the comment, "Who is this guy Bruce Merz? And why is all of Christendom praying for him?"

Chapter Eight

Bruce loves his brother Mark. Mark loves Bruce. They just haven't always been able to figure out their relationship, and it has been through many strained seasons. On Monday night as a group of men took turns standing around Bruce's bed praying into the wee hours, I heard that Mark felt he needed to reconcile with Bruce. I don't know the details, nor do I think that I am supposed to, I only know that it must have been a beautiful scene to behold.

What happened with Mark was apparently something God wanted to do in many people's hearts. It seemed to be the first fruits and even a catalyst for a movement led by the Holy Spirit to restore relationships. Here are just some samples that came to me via Facebook (names changed):

> Denis: *I don't know if anyone else is experiencing this, but as I pray for Bruce and Lara, God has been bringing up little offenses that I've put away over the years. Things that "don't matter" because I never see any of these people. But now I am standing with them praying for something way bigger than my own hurts or injustices. These "little" things stand in the way of my ability to war with my whole heart! Jesus is so amazing, caring about every detail...affecting the hearts of those interceding. Finish the work, Daddy, complete wholeness for Bruce and the Body!*

While He Lay Dying

Janine: *God is dealing with offense in my heart, and I fully believe what you and Bruce are walking through is a beautiful picture of what God is doing in the Body of Christ. He is bringing us all back together. Reminding us that our petty divisions and judgments are stupid in the face of what is really important, fighting together and seeing God's kingdom come. The walls of division are completely blurred when our hearts join together because we love Bruce and want to see him thrive. I believe you are ushering a new movement in the Body of Christ where critical thinking and judgment falls away and we join together for the greater fight, the fight that matters. You and Bruce and your family's lives are a prophetic picture. I believe as we let offense fall away the Body is healed.*

Maria: *During the first weeks of Bruce being at the hospital in this condition, God brought conviction into my heart to repent for not valuing the people that he puts around me for seasons in my life. For a long time I did not make phone calls to my mom in law to talk to her because I was upset at her for the way that she is with us. However that is not an excuse I have to bless her and not be selfish. So I started calling her to know how she is doing and she also started to call me. I have forgiven her and removed the offense from my heart that I had against her.*

Kendra: *During this time I have learned again what it means by praying unceasingly. I feel that although there is at this time struggles between our staff, your illness, Bruce, has united everyone. The petty differences are forgotten as we focus on the common goal of praying for your healing.*

And there were many more. It is amazing what happens when people begin to pray, when we make every effort to be diligent, to pray from the heart and not give up, and to lean in hard to pray, then we begin to hear the Lord about our own lives too! I was seriously excited to see what the Lord was doing and I was asking Him myself if there was anyone who I needed to reconcile with.

And then an old friend came to mind. I sent her a message letting her know that I missed her. I missed her friendship. I am not sure what happened in that relationship. We once were very close, but I know I had begun to grow bitter that she didn't seem to want me in her life anymore. The bitterness was the result of not dealing with my hurt feelings and for the sadness of losing my dear friend. When we met, I simply told her that I loved her and missed her. We ended up spending some time together at the hospital, and all that bitterness was washed away and replaced with friendship again. It is good to follow the Lord's leading and do things that feel scary. It is so freeing to forgive and be forgiven!

Meanwhile, even more people started praying. The Lord began to stir in the hearts of the Body of Christ. People we didn't know were burdened to the point of weeping for Bruce and our family. Over the next days and weeks we heard from hundreds of churches across Canada and the United States who were praying for us. Some prayed during their services, some fasted and prayed, some met in home groups to pray for a man no one in the group even knew. One group up north in Grande Prairie, Alberta was apparently praying for two men with flesh-eating disease: one was a guy named Bruce, and the other was an online math teacher named Mr. Merz! They were praying for him twice having heard the request from two separate sources! These people came from Anglican, Presbyterian, Alliance, Brethren, Four Square, Baptist, Lutheran, Evangelical Free, Mennonite, Pentecostal, and non-denominational churches! It didn't seem to matter what people's backgrounds were, the Lord was moving in hearts and mobilizing the troops so to speak, to pray for Bruce!

Chapter Nine

Day 4–Tuesday

Tuesday was filled with ups and downs. First, his kidneys deteriorated to their worst state yet. Kidney function is measured by how well they are filtering the blood. The lab tested his creatinine levels. A normal person has a level of 80 to 120. Something in the low one hundreds would be reasonable for someone Bruce's size. His was at 534 that day! Consequently, they immediately hooked him up to a dialysis machine and kept it on 24/7. This acted as his kidneys and took the pressure off of them so they might have a chance to regenerate and recuperate.

Some very scary problems began to show up in his blood work too. His platelet count was 7, whereas a normal platelet count is 150 or higher. This meant that he was at an *extremely* high risk for bleeding out or bleeding internally. Conversely, due to the effects of the sepsis, he was also at an extremely high risk for blood clotting. Truth be told, just lying in a bed without moving puts a person at higher risk for clotting, not to mention what the sepsis was doing to his blood. Unfortunately because of his severely low platelet count, they were unable to give him blood thinners. Basically, he could have died at any moment from either a blood clot or from bleeding out, and they couldn't give medicine for either condition since it would likely cause the other to occur. His body became a ticking time bomb.

His blood pressure didn't seem to be as low as it was the day before but was still a great concern. It was like this disease was eating him alive from the inside out. Necrotizing fasciitis is ravenous and insatiable. His blood was poisoned, his organs failing, his lungs labouring, his heart was racing, his blood pressure without meds was virtually non-existent, and he had next to no circulation to his extremities.

Yet, through all of this I had hope, a hope that is hard to even explain. In my heart I knew that he would not die. He just wouldn't. It didn't make sense to me that he would die now. I thought back to how the Lord had brought us together in his perfect timing, and I just couldn't see how that could end after only six short years. Nothing of his death made sense to me, so I never dwelled on that thought for too long. Fear did not grip me. Hope did. And that hope had to be from God because what I saw in front of me with my eyes and the reports I heard with my ears offered no hope.

There were times when I went to that place of "what-if" for the sake of my children and began to ask myself what my plan was if I was wrong about Bruce living. It was so unbelievably hard to picture any kind of a life without him, but I felt like I needed a plan for the sake of my little ones if I was wrong. Those were sad times, but the Lord truly protected me from fear. In my heart I knew that he would live.

His parents believed it too. My wonderful father-in-law, Fred, has so much faith. When people returned to the house with discouraging reports, he would say, "We will speak only the truth about God's plans for Bruce. No negative worry." My parents also had a deep assurance that their son-in-love, as Mom calls him, would live, although my mother wondered at times if the test of faith would go as far as trusting for him to be raised from the dead. His brother and his cousins were certain of it, and Bishop Todd said he was 100 percent sure Bruce would live through this. The other pastors at River of Life and many friends felt sure of it too, but we also realized we had a fight on our hands.

Interestingly, we were never asked to make a decision about amputating his leg or any other parts (a frequent outcome of flesh-eating disease). I have heard that it was discussed amongst the medical specialists, but it was never spoken of to me. I can only speculate as to why. I also want to make it clear, that even with such faith, I never at any point refused medical help or suggestions for Bruce.

I don't know much about death, and I won't pretend to be a theologian on the matter. I do know this: we all die. I will die one day, Bruce will die one day, and our children will even die eventually. But everything in me screamed that this was not Bruce's time to die! This disease was so clearly demonic to anyone watching. It was eating him and attacking him, trying to kill him before his time. The enemy wanted to stop whatever God intends Bruce to be and do. However, as much as the presence of the enemy was obvious and apparent, the hand of God was ever more apparent and ten times stronger and more present!

There were so many times when people walked into Bruce's room and felt the thick, thick presence of the Lord. Many would describe his room as an open heaven. "It's like you can pray without filters or distractions," one person said. It felt easy to connect with God and to hear His voice there.

The reports of visions of angels started pouring in. Some said they saw guardian angels at the door to his room, some said healing angels, but often it was worshipping angels singing over his body. Children drew pictures of angels they saw when they prayed for him. People from around the world sent me stories of angel dreams and visions while praying for him. Nearly all of the stories of visions and dreams I received from believers were about angels or seeing Jesus by Bruce's side or cradling my dear husband's head in His hands and kissing him. Here is just one:

> Kyra: *Tonight we were worshipping and I can't remember the song, but I looked around the sanctuary of the church and where there were empty seats and spaces there were angels and they were worshipping and all with one voice. It was amazing and spectacular! Then I saw Bruce in the hospital bed. And he was sitting up and his room was filled with angels too! They were singing the same song we were singing at church. And it was like because as a church body we stood (and stand) with you*

guys that we created this tie to each other...Like an invisible chain that
we could feed through. And I didn't hear the words I just felt that God
was saying that when we stand together as brothers we are one...And
even the angels sing the same song.

Later that afternoon, when I was out in the waiting room with
about 20 or so friends and family, Bruce's nurse came to me and
kneeled in front of me. His eyes were wet, and his lip trembled.

"Lara," he said, "Listen. During the dressing change we found
something. It looks like it may be another spot of infected tissue. We've
called the surgeon to come have a look..."

You know it isn't good news when it brings tears to the eyes of an
experienced intensive care nurse. Oh, my heart just plummeted. I
knew how hard the first surgery was on Bruce, and I couldn't imagine
him handling another one much better. I went and sat on the floor in
the hall by myself and wept for my husband. So much sadness was in
my heart. I waited there for an hour or so until the nurse found me to
tell me that the surgeon wasn't concerned and that for now it looked
okay. Oh the rollercoaster!

Chapter Ten

We hadn't seen any significant breakthrough yet, so once again, remembering the lessons the Lord had already taught me, I felt we needed to focus on thanksgiving. So I posted on Facebook, asking people to give thanks with me. Here are just some of the responses I saw, something I'm truly, truly grateful for! (Some names have been changed to protect privacy.)

Dan: *I am thankful for how God is showing His great love for Bruce through the Body, the family of Christ. His love is miraculous, life changing, and life giving!*

Sharron: *Thankful for his laugh, for how fast he talks (looking forward to hearing it again soon!), thankful for his faith, for the impact he, his teaching, his praying has had on G and I and our boys, thankful that he makes math look so cool, thankful for his generosity, and that big problems mean big miracles. Love you all, thankful for you all.*

Rochelle: *I've never even met Bruce, and haven't seen you, Lara, in years...but the outpouring of love and prayer that I see for you two speaks volumes alone. I'm thankful for the support you and your family must feel during this difficult time. (Philippians 4:6, Do not be anxious about anything, but in every situation, by prayer and petition, with thanksgiving, present your requests to God.)*

Darlene: *Thank You, Jesus for holding Bruce and Lara and their family closer to you during this time! Thank You for Your healing power, Your plan for their future, and Your presence in their lives!*

Erin: *I...have yet to meet you, Lara, but have always looked up to Bruce. He is a true man of God, and I am thankful that he met and married such a strong woman as you. Watching this situation unfold and seeing how many lives the two of you have touched has been amazing. God is not done with Bruce yet, and this is just going to be another miracle that Bruce will be able to add to his testimony! This is also going to influence your children as they see a very tangible and physical way that God can move, and they will see the support that you have been shown as well...your children are blessed to have such strong parents. This situation is going to change lives and good will come from this! We believe!!*

Emmy: *I am thankful for his heart, a beautiful big heart for seeing the fullness of God's kingdom come. I love how he loves to worship and pray, and how his prayers really do change things. He is an amazing leader and father to many. Just thinking about him makes me smile. I love his wacky sense of humour and his ability to eat large amounts of chocolate! My life is better having Bruce Merz as a part of it. Thank you Jesus!*

Tara: *I am thankful that over the years the Merz family has given God all the glory for their miracles, not passing anything off as fluke, luck or man's efforts. I am thankful that even in this excruciating and frightening time, Jesus is still being lifted high in their lives and light is being shone into the darkness. Not just for them, but for any who doubt in the greatness of God.*

Rebecca: *You guys have been through so many miracles on the last few years I believe this is our next one! We will declare Bruce is the healed of the Lord! I got to know Bruce a little better one day at preschool registration. It was so nice to have someone to talk to when we all had to get up early to register our kids. :)*

Bruce and Lara Merz

Robyn: *I am so thankful for our friendship. Both you and Bruce have always been such a wonderful encouragement to Aaron and I; we love you and are praying for incredible things for your family!*

Jacqueline: *So many things I'm thankful for, thankful for a family that proclaims the truth of the Father, who love and enjoy life. Thankful that Bruce always pushes to pursue deeper the presence of God and spur others to this place and that he just enjoys life while he does. I am thankful for the work of Jesus that allows us to dwell as sons and daughters with the most high God, and that through this work we can receive the abundant and free flowing Spirit that brings all good things. I am thankful for YOU, Lara, a woman of God who builds up her home with your words of faith. We love you guys.*

Kristy: *Thank You, Jesus, for Your unending, steadfast love. Thank You, Jesus, for Your mercies that never come to an end. They are new every morning. Thank You, Jesus, for Your faithfulness. Thank You, Jesus, that we overcome by the blood of the Lamb and the word of our testimony. Thank You, Jesus, for Bruce and. Lara and the wonderful testimony that they have for You. I thank You, Jesus, that the Merz family serves You and that it is apparent by their testimony. Thank You, Jesus, that You are the same yesterday, today and forever. We praise You, Jesus.*

Amos: *I'm so thankful for Bruce's impact in my life! For his humour, the amazing speed that he can talk, the amount of e-mails he can send in a day, and his ever positive, encouraging attitude! For his great teaching ability and his commitment to spur people on to greatness. Bruce is great at that! I remember Bruce teaching about group prayer one time—each person has wonderful things to pray about on a personal level; but God has something special for this group, today; so lay any agenda down and let's try to find it together! This is a great principle, one that requires humility, but enables great unity and opens the door for corporate encounters of God's presence! I'm thankful that Bruce is an agent of unity in the Church, and that has never been more evident than it is right now. I'm thankful that the Church has been called to prayer. I'm thankful that God is stirring up faith in his people and*

63

that at the center of it all is a man and a family that has more faith for miracles than anyone I know. I'm thankful that I serve a merciful, gracious, and compassionate God. A God who heals, and a God who loves us all deeply. Above all, I'm thankful for the victory won at the cross of Christ and the gift of the Spirit that Jesus pours out on His people. Christus Victor!!

Jean: *I was thrilled when Bruce entered your life, Lara; I know how much having a family meant to you and how you were struggling with the idea that God may not have that in the cards for you. I am so thankful that Bruce lives in a country where medical care is provided without fear of financial consequences and that he has friends who speak "medicalese" who are advocating for him and ensuring that the best methods and strategies are being employed. We are praying for you all! Please let us know if there is anything we can do.*

Peter: *I am so thankful for Bruce's passion, integrity, and sensitive spirit. He has taught me so much both personally and professionally. He was my math practicum supervisor, and I watched, in awe, as he had students eating out of his hands! They had so much respect for him and held him with such regard. Bruce, I'm looking forward to hanging with you again!*

Sandra: *I am so thankful for you and Bruce. For the great love that you showed for me and the other interns. It was absolutely visible how much Bruce cared about us and how much he desired for us to encounter the Father. I am thankful for Bruce's huge heart and for the excitement with which both of you love to share of God's grace and goodness and miracles in your life. I am so thankful for your faith! Your great faith leads others to have faith for things they didn't know how to believe for before. Praise the Lord! Jesus makes all things new! Praise the Lord, the Father holds all things in His hands! Praise The Lord the Father holds His son Bruce in His hands!*

Hannah: *I am thankful for the global community of God-loving people that have been brought together to battle in prayer for your wonderful family. If anything, THAT is inspiring and beautiful.*

Aaron: *I am thankful for Bruce's serving heart, his warm personality and how when he gets excited he rapidly speaks his thoughts. He never fails to say "hi" even when he is in a rush and has always had time to find out what has been going on in my life. I am thankful for knowing such a wonderful man of God, a father, and husband to his family and above all for his friendship.*

Jeni: *I thank the Lord for Bruce, he is an awesome man of God, exemplary husband and father~ who is such a motivator and a gift of encouragement to those of us on the mission field and beyond! THE LORD IS WITH YOU, BRUCE, HE IS MIGHTY TO SAVE!!!*

Raquel: *Father, thank You for Jesus. Thank You that by His Stripes we are healed. Thank You for preserving Bruce's physical body, mind and spirit. I bless him in Jesus' name.*

Melinda: *I have been thinking about this all night, just what I am thankful for. Jesus, I am thankful for Your life, death, resurrection, and ascension. I am overwhelmed with Your love for us and deeply moved to be lifting up our brother Bruce in this holy week, even as we remember Your cross. I am so thankful for the way You have defeated every enemy and brought every struggle to submission under Your power. I am thankful for Bruce and Lara! I'm so blessed by their love for me, their acceptance, and the way they pour into my life. I'm thankful for peace, for hope, for the Spirit whose presence fills our lives with these things and so much more!*

Danean: *I am thankful that Jesus bore all our sickness and diseases on the cross so that we might have life! This is what we have been claiming and thanking Jesus for Bruce. As we prayed today and placed Bruce at the foot of the cross, I saw a picture of Jesus' life-giving blood dripping onto Bruce. I'm thankful for one of a kind miracles. He cares for our every need.*

And that was just a taste of the many, many posts! For myself, I had learned there is always something to be thankful for and I knew that even if Bruce died, God is still good. I felt so much trust in Him. I couldn't imagine what life would be like without Bruce, but no matter what happened, God would take care of us, and there would *always* be things to be thankful for.

While He Lay Dying

That night Bishop Todd and about five other staff members, church elders, and friends who love Bruce were anointing him with oil and praying for him (James 5:14) when Todd turned to the nurse and asked her what miracle she wanted to see first. She said the most important thing she saw a need for right now was an improvement in his blood pressure.

This started the most amazing trend. Now all of a sudden the huge miracle we were asking God for was broken down into smaller miracles. It was significant because it gave people specific things to pray for, but most importantly it showed us that if our faith was not big enough for the whole miracle of seeing him completely restored, breaking it into bite-sized pieces made it easier to pray according to the measure of faith people did have. One of the guys came out from Bruce's room and asked us in the waiting room to pray with them for the same thing, so we tacked up a big sign that said: *Miracle #1 Blood Pressure.*

The whole waiting room concentrated on praying for his blood pressure. Messages were sent to all the home prayer groups that were warring for him, and we all began praying for his blood pressure. Specifically the nurse wanted his mean arterial pressure number to increase to indicate that he was holding at a certain level, and then they could drop the medicine a bit and see if it stabilized. It had been hovering around 55 for the past few days, which was lower than they wanted, even with the high dose of meds he was on. (Normal range is about 70 to 110, but over 60 is generally enough to perfuse vital organs for the average person.) So we all started praying and praying and praying. And the numbers started changing! They were going up, and staying up, even after 20 minutes! The nurse dropped the med one step down, and it held strong at 70! So we prayed more, and it went up to 74! The nurse couldn't believe what she was watching. She was still skeptical but certainly surprised.

Other nurses were starting to pop their heads in his room to see what was happening. After a while, they were having a hard time hiding their giddiness!

He held at the next level too, so they did another drop! Every time the nurse dropped the dosage of the medication, the guys in his room texted the people in the waiting room and everyone erupted in cheering. Someone let the prayer groups at homes know, and *they* erupted in cheering! He needed to drop many more times, but it was exhilarating to watch!

It was honestly the very first time since Bruce had been admitted that I heard the word "improvement." It was music to my ears and to my heart! Hope and excitement soared. We must have looked like a bunch of crazy people! Here we were hooting and jumping up and down late into the night for a man who was still in *seriously* critical condition, but it didn't matter because we grabbed on to every single improvement and found so much hope in it! We could *see* God working!

I stayed that night until 4:00 am. I was so ready to see him jump out of that bed and come home! I guess I got a bit ahead of myself, but I was simply so happy because I knew it was going to happen. I didn't know how or when, but I knew it was going to happen.

More and more people were hearing about Bruce, and even though there are many worthy causes folks are asked to pray for all the time, for some reason this request for one man in a tiny hospital room in a small city in Canada caught their attention and they felt drawn to pray. The Lord was moving on hearts and mobilizing the troops. Here are just a few more examples of that:

* The local Christian radio station prayed for Bruce on air and posted the updates on their website.

* The Christian radio station in Edmonton, six hours north of us, was doing the same.

* 10,000 of the God TV intercessors were praying.

* The Billy Graham Association of Canada prayer team was praying.

* The Miracle Channel intercessors were praying.

* We had reports of prayer coming from China, India, Thailand, Laos, Vietnam, Mongolia, South Africa, Kenya, Uganda, Zambia, The Gambia, New Zealand, England, Columbia, Mexico, Nunavut, Germany, Australia, Mexico, the

While He Lay Dying

Dominican Republic, the Turks and Caicos, Scotland, the Philippines, South Korea, and literally coast to coast in Canada and the USA!

This is when I realized that something bigger than us and our little family was going on here. God was raising up an army!

That night my post on Facebook was about what had happened in the ICU room, and it changed the way I did Facebook posts from then on. Now every time I posted, I told everyone what we were all praying for that day. And thousands of people joined hand in hand around the world to pray for the same thing—*the same small miracle.*

I have seen miracles in my life, some for me, and some for strangers. I have seen the deaf prayed for and healed, the crippled walk, drug addicts instantly released from their addictions and more. I knew that God could heal Bruce in an instant. In fact, at the beginning that is what I was waiting for, but God had something different in mind. He had the world watching, an entire hospital watching, a city watching. He wanted people to journey with us, to fight and not give up after a couple of prayers. He wanted us to pray and then see the answers, over and over again, to remind His Body that *He hears our prayers and He answers them.*

I received many emails and stories from people who had just about given up on God hearing their prayers until this. Now they felt that God heard them. Here are a few of those:

Jackie: *I have been following the updates on Bruce through the CKVN website and have been praying for him with my kids before school. When I read that you had asked for testimonies on what God has been doing through this situation in the lives of others, I dismissed it. This morning as I thought, I cried a bit. Lara, I marvel at the grace and strength with which you are walking through this, and I have been blessed! I guess I don't really have a lot to share except that you have touched my heart. I was just talking to my dad at Christmas about how I don't really see the effects of my prayers. It seemed like everyone my kids and I prayed for either stayed sick or died. This morning was a realization that our prayers are making a difference in someone's life. I know it's not just our prayers but your faith and perseverance has restored something that I had lost...and the knowing that prayer can move mountains!*

Even though we live in the same city and I have never met you, we are connected by faith in Jesus Christ. Thank you for your example!

David: *I would like to share what the Lord has done through this:*
1. I had to quit my job in January due to some reasons. Because it's a big issue being unemployed, I felt a heavy burden on my heart crying to God for a new job. However when we started to pray for Bruce, I realized that this is a much bigger issue because it's a life-or-death struggle. Some days later while continue to pray for Bruce, I realized that I had nearly forgotten that I'm out of work! My burden regarding a new job was gone! And encouraged by the good news and what God was doing in Bruce's body I received a strong confidence that God will also handle my "little problem" and give me a new job. So I am excited to see how everything will turn out all right.
2. While praying for Bruce at our church on Easter Sunday, one person received an impression from God that He is taking illness out of Bruce and putting healthiness inside instead! It was a great encouragement for us to know that God will give a positive answer to our prayer.
3. I believe in divine healing. In the past I thought it may happen or not because it depends on God's sovereignty. But now God showed me that He really wants to do what we ask for! We are His children and while associating with Him, He shares His thoughts and opinions with us. If we pray on this basis, He will answer!
4. While looking on prayer as described above, God's answer isn't limited at all. He is able to do ANYTHING! Luke 18:27 says, "What is impossible with man is possible with God." That's just awesome!

Krista: *The last 10 months have been quite trying for me. I got married almost a year ago (which has been great!) but in the last year there have been other life changes including moving, starting new jobs, finding a new church family, and selling a house. We are currently walking through some testing times, but the Lord has used your journey of sickness and healing to deeply root truth in my heart. In the last number of months I've had times of serious doubt that God is listening to my prayers, and if He is, why are the answers seeming so distant and unsteady? For the first time in a long time I've felt like God has heard me and is answering. But more than learning the basic truth, truth that God answers prayers (such a simple yet life-changing truth!) is that I am coming to know the truth that Christ does not merely answer prayers but that He, Himself, is the answer. He does not just give healing, but He is healing. This is being burned on my heart daily, and when I've been tempted to be overwhelmed by life I am reminded that Bruce is continually being healed. In the same way that Bruce is being healed of a physical illness, I am being healed of a spiritual illness. He is a loving and faithful Father!*

Mel: *Just as I'm wondering why or how I'm still awake, I read a Bruce update, or reflect on this week, and I remember the amazing things that are happening in Bruce and all of us. I've never been so drawn to prayer. I've slept three of the last 40 hours, but I really just want to be at the hospital praying and praising.*

Wow.

Bruce had a dream of seeing our church engaged in 24/7 prayer. Now here, in the waiting room of the local hospital, one of his former interns started a sign-up sheet just to organize the efforts and to spread everyone out. Almost immediately, the time slots for the next three weeks were filled in! Moms of small children signed up for midnight to 2:00 am every night, and grandmothers signed up for 4:00 am every day! It was amazing!

Groups meeting regularly were learning to hear the voice of God and getting so excited. One person would feel the Lord impress a verse on their hearts, and three other people would have the same verse written down. It was so fun to watch the excitement people felt about prayer and hearing what God was doing! Many of the groups delved deeply into corporate prayer, hearing the Holy Spirit and praying what was on the Lord's heart to pray.

My brother, Chris, and his wife, Shellie (who came to be with us from out of town), felt the call to do a prayer walk around the hospital seven times each day. When they left and went back home, they continued to walk seven kilomètres everyday without fail, interceding for Bruce's healing!

A couple of separate groups found the Lord leading them to pray for the country and repent for the sins of our country, all on the same night! I had tears in my eyes as I kept thinking, "Bruce would *love* this! This is exactly what he longed to see for so long!"

Bruce also had a heart for unity among the denominations. In our city we had pastors from different churches and denominations coming to his bedside together to pray for him. No one was arguing about the doctrine of healing and how to go about it; everyone was just praying as they knew how and as they were led to. It was truly beautiful!

People were not only learning how to pray again, but also realizing that God heard *their* prayers! They were learning about His character and power and about themselves in the process! Their faith was growing.

You may remember that when Bruce first came to River of Life church to work there, he was striving to see God do all of the things that he felt passionate about. He saw few results then, but it was almost comical to see that so many of the things that were near to Bruce's heart were being birthed and were flourishing, not just in our church but in churches around the world. If only Bruce were awake to see it!

I loved what was happening with children too! Bruce has a way with kids. He makes each one feel special, happy, and secure. He is a teacher through and through, all the time. He never misses an opportunity to teach something to a child. At the time he became ill he was teaching a catechism class to a group of kids who were preparing for baptism. He had also spent a number of years teaching the junior-high-aged youth to hear God's voice, as well as spending time playing on the carpet with our own two toddlers and all their little friends in the two's and three's room on Sunday morning. All children who knew him dearly loved him!

These children rose up and fought for his life! Some begged their parents morning, noon and night to keep praying for Bruce! One toddler, just barely talking, kept walking around the house saying, "Pray for Bruce!" Some of our friends' kids recited memory verses and constantly ask for updates on Bruce so they could pray for him. That moved me so much! Seeing the little people rise up and pray and fight like an army has always been a dream of ours. But I know that in spirit they were no "little" army, but rather a force to be reckoned with. Kids do not receive a junior version of the Holy Spirit. In a way, I was not surprised to hear of the children from our church praying for Bruce. It was hearing about children from other cities that shocked me.

Sherri: *When we started to pray for Bruce, we told our kids what was happening and they wanted to join with us to pray. We had told them that Mr. Bruce was a friend of Mommy's from years ago, and that he was very sick and in the hospital and had a wife and kids that loved him very much and wanted him to get better and come back home to them. We told them he was very sick, and needed Jesus to heal his body very much. I didn't realize the impact this was having on them until one night, when I was tucking Elisha into bed for the night. Her words that night just burned into my head.*

She got very quiet, and then asked me, "Mommy, does Mr. Bruce have a bed?"

"Yes." I said, "a very special bed in the hospital for him to sleep on."

"And does he have 'fishes'?" (She has a favourite blanket that has fishes on it, so she was really asking, "Does Mr. Bruce have a special blanket?")

I said, "Yes, they have given him special blankets so he is warm to sleep."

"Does he have a Mommy to stay by his bed?"

"Well," I said, "he has doctors and doctor's helpers that are with him all through the night to help him."

Then she asked a question that just broke my heart. "Mommy, do Daddies break sometimes?"

My heart was rattled. "Yes...sometimes they do" was all I could say for the first moment. Then she said, " Mommy, can we please pray that my Daddy doesn't break?!"

I could hardly speak, let alone pray at first. So, we prayed for my little girl's Daddy, and then she asked me five times to pray for Mr. Bruce! I think she all of the sudden really empathized with your kids and what they must be feeling in some way. My little girl absolutely adores her Daddy, and she knew that Mr. Bruce was a Daddy, so he had kids that absolutely adored him, too. It all hit her big, little heart so hard.

Our six year old has also been reminding us to pray for Bruce often throughout the day. This experience has really taught our kids what it means to pray without ceasing, to keep others lifted up before God, no matter what's going on around us. And they have prayed in simple solid faith, believing God for a miracle each time! It has challenged and strengthened my own faith. Gabriel told me a few days ago, that we must pray at each meal for Mr. Bruce, until he is home from the hospital.

Susan: *The kids and I are praying with passion and conviction for Bruce, you and the kids. God hears our prayers and listens intently—particularly to those of children...We love you!*

Nick: *Praying here in Kelowna for complete healing for Bruce and strength for Lara and the kids...This morning our daughter (five) was praying for Bruce..."Jesus we fire sickness out of Bruce's body and speak full healing into him." We believe God to be glorified through this whole process.*

Kathy: *Know that we are praying! I shared what is happening with my children—Ben was weeping as he prayed for your family—that Bruce would live and not die, and that you would trust God (which I know you are) whatever happens.*

Although I know some of these adults, some of their children have never met Bruce themselves. God is so amazing.

It would seem that all of the things of God that were dear to Bruce, that he strived to accomplish for years, were all coming to fruition. And he was asleep for the whole thing! Isn't that just like God? He puts the dreams and passions in our hearts, but we don't need to strive to make them happen, we just need to partner with God and He will make them happen. In this case, all Bruce had to do was sleep in the Father's arms and He broadcast Bruce's heart all over the world!

Chapter Eleven

Day 5—Wednesday

Facebook update:

So I went home at 4am last night and the waiting room still had many who were staying the whole night to pray. I just called his nurse for the update and this is what he said, "He is not over the hump yet but he is moving in the right direction." In less than 12 hours he has gone from 2.3 on the main blood pressure med down to 1.3!! and the other blood pressure med was down from 2.4 to 1.8!!!!! The levels that indicate how his kidneys are doing went from 534 to 460ish (a smaller number is a better number)!!! So he is slowly improving!!

Please keep praying for his feet. The nurse said that before the purple yucky look was going up his legs and now his legs are pink and fine but there is still a lot of concern about whether he is getting enough circulation to his feet because the meds were so high for so long. They've improved slightly but we need lots of prayer! The nurse said he might lose some toes but I refuse to agree with that and will pray that his feet will turn pink again. (All I can think is that big guys fall over without toes, so he needs these!!) PLEASE PRAY WITH ME! Let's get him off the meds completely and have his feet back to normal colour! He still needs to pee more and he

While He Lay Dying

is still on life support and there are a lot more improvements we need before
he is out of the woods, but I can see and feel God at work so I am not in
the least bit discouraged!! Please keep praying and expecting and antici-
pating that with each report we can celebrate a little!

So overnight, when the men (and everyone in the waiting rooms
and prayer groups) were praying, his blood pressure medication
dosage was dropped by a half! Thank You, Jesus! His body was finally
doing something! He wasn't stable yet, and wasn't out of the woods, but
I cannot even tell you how exciting it was to see his body respond, even
in the littlest way! Still, there was the concern of his feet.

I later heard that the nurses had been making ongoing predictions
all along about whether he would keep his toes or lose them, and most
thought that he would lose them. I went to the end of his bed and felt
them. They were like ice. His legs and feet were dark purple from his
calf down to his toes, which were pure white, stiff, and cold. The toes
felt like they might snap if I held them too tightly (which I later found
out was actually true).

Somehow standing there holding those cold feet in my hands, I just
knew it; I knew that this was the last day for these toes and feet. If he
didn't have full circulation restored to them soon, they would not survive. I am not a doctor, I don't even know that medically it was a fact
that they had another day, but I do know that my spirit was screaming
it, and all the doctors and nurses were constantly checking them and
putting in their opinions about whether they were going to need
amputation. We later found out that one of our friends who asked a
nurse how bad his feet really were had it spelled out for him. "In 24
hours his toes will start falling off."

It was really in conjunction with the blood pressure and reducing
the medication and was still the first miracle we were praying for, but I
pushed hard for those toes! We spread the word that we were praying
for pink toes! There was a sense of urgency to this prayer as many of us
felt there was little time left.

Our prayer group of thousands (tens of thousands now) around
the world got on it, and so did our group in the hospital, as well as the
groups meeting in homes and at the church! That night all of the

elders from our church took turns going into Bruce's room to pray for him and for his toes. I came into the waiting room and saw more people there than I had seen yet.

Sometimes it shocked me to see so many people crying—people I didn't know thought so highly of Bruce or loved him so deeply. I felt profoundly proud to be married to such an incredible man, who has touched so many. The truth is that many of us never get to see this in our lives. Doesn't it seem so often that people never show their real feelings until after someone dies? If you could go to your own funeral you might be shocked to see just how many people love you and have been touched by you in some way. We just had the blessing of witnessing this without the funeral!

In fact, because I tended to have difficult pregnancies with nine months of nausea and vomiting and painful hip joints and other problems and then had C-sections, I had spent much of the previous year in bed. Bruce (and the grandmas) picked up the slack with the house and kids. You can't isolate yourself for that long without feeling a loss of relationship. It's no fault of anyone, but after having our newest baby girl, we pulled our heads out of the sand and looked around for friends and felt like people had moved on without us. Just weeks before this disease hit, Bruce wondered aloud who our close friends were anymore. It is so easy to feel isolated when you isolate yourself, isn't it? We did it out of necessity, but people will move on if you never leave your house. It's no fault of theirs. You have to work at getting back into their circles and connect with friends again. *Out of sight, out of mind,* I thought.

But here I was in a waiting room filled with red-eyed people who would do anything for that man! I laughed and thought, "Oh if Bruce could only see this, he would never doubt we had close friends again! He would wonder how he was possibly going to juggle all of these amazing friends!" It also made me realize that we wait too long. Why do we wait until a funeral or life and death crisis to let people we love know just how much we love them? Why do we hesitate to let them know what kind of impact they have made on us? What good will it do after death? Why are we too shy to love and honour others unabashedly?

I am equally guilty of this! I take people and relationships for granted and forget that so many of us need reassurance of where we stand. So many of us walk around wondering if people really like us or if we have ever made any kind of an impression on others in our lives and never get the answer to that. I was blessed to hear it and to see it and let it sink into me. It shouldn't be like that! I started telling everyone without shame or fear just how much he or she meant to me! I was so touched to see people doing this with each other too. I was blown away with how the macho man walls broke down when I saw men hugging each other, and saying, "I love you, man," to their buddies, to me, and to Bruce! Some of his buddies massaged his feet while they were praying for him. They sang over him too. No pride, just love.

We started a journal in the waiting room: "For Bruce When He Wakes Up." Even the guys poured their hearts out and told him just how special he was to them. I knew my husband, and I knew that this would be exactly what his heart longed to hear from his buddies. There is no shame in loving deeply and being open about that. That is how true and deep friendship is secured. Our hearts were knitted so closely with so many through this experience!

This was my nightly report that night:

Ok so here is the nightly update (sorry it is so late).

For most of the day his blood pressure stayed the same, but all the nurses and doctors were excited to see "improvement" (my new favourite word). It is funny how exciting it can be just to dial back some meds, despite the fact that he is still on life support. But when you see God start to move you know that it's like making a snowball and things are just going to get bigger and pick up speed!

Main prayer concerns:

* *Still the BP is the #1 thing we are looking for, he really needs to be completely off all those meds and doing it himself.*
* *His platelets are low (7), normal is 150 (I think). They are okay with it as long as the count is above 10. This morning it was 15 and now it is 7 so it is officially the only thing that is going in backward motion for us. So, they gave him some platelets tonight and we will pray that that will help them too.*
* *His feet still need to be pink!*

* *Kidneys need to start functioning on their own (start peeing better).*
* *He has also developed pneumonia now as well.*
* *Please pray also for my kids, they are starting to miss Daddy and me. And I need to learn to figure out how to be there and here and making sure they are secure and have their tanks full.*
* *Pray that I will sleep well tonight and start to be able to eat again.*

Praise (this is my favourite part, I leave it to last because this is the part I want to linger in your hearts and minds (and mine) after you read this:

* *His BP drugs are down from 2.3, and 2.4 when we started going specifically after it to 0.9 and 1.6!!!!!!!!!!!!!!!!!!!! Consider that they usually only drop by 0.1 or 0.2 at a time that makes for a lot of drops!! And not many more to go! I want to wake up to him being off those drugs and doing that on his own.*
* *A lot of his blood work is showing some good signs.*
* *His kidney numbers are slowly but surely getting better, and he is peeing a little bit on his own.*
* *This one is my favourite surprise I think: his hands and arms are soft and warm! They have been weird and cold and clammy and hard like rocks. Now his hands feel great and healthy!*
* *His toes on the left are getting purple and the foot has a more distinguishable pulse than before, and the ones on the right are a little bit better too. You can feel warmth on his calves and then on his ankles and then just on the nearest part on his foot. There was no warmth there at all this morning!*
* *The Lord is moving in so many more people than Bruce and I, people are going through their own journeys with God and that is sooooo cool! Open your heart and let God move in places in you too. He is a safe and gentle God so just trust Him and go for the ride. I know He is working so much in me too.*

Bless you all for your devotion, love, steadfastness, and valiant fighting. You have all humbled me and shown me the Father's love in ways you will never know. Thank you.

While He Lay Dying

My kids were handling things fairly well, given the situation, but they needed prayer. Their emotions were understandably all over the place. The effectiveness of prayer for them was so obvious. Vivia had a blocked tear duct that caused her eyelid to swell and left red irritated patches of skin around her eye and on her cheek. Dried secretions built up and glued her eyelashes together. She needed it to be cleaned with a cotton swab and warm sterile water and to have drops put in several times a day. After we asked people to specifically pray for the children, we heard her making happy baby noises in her bassinet one morning. She smiled and cooed as her ten-year old cousin, Arianna, who loves babies and was there with her family to help, picked her up. Vivia's eye was healed. The swelling was gone and even the red irritated skin around her eye was perfectly normal!

One evening the children seemed particularly upset and were being very naughty for their grandmothers. As we posted a prayer request for their little hearts on Facebook, people responded immediately, and very shortly afterward the children were playing quietly and cheerfully and were soon sleeping peacefully.

There were times, however, when no one but Daddy would do when it came to consoling little Axel. One afternoon he was not feeling well, and to add insult to injury his sister shut him out of her room, and then he hurt himself tumbling off the kitchen counter (where he ought not to have been). He was just having a bad day. I happened to be coming in the door, as I often slipped back to the house to put him down for his nap. My brother had not been able to comfort him; Bruce's brother couldn't comfort him; I couldn't even comfort him. I held him and rocked him in the big chair, but tears ran down from his big brown eyes. He cried in a loud voice, "I want my Daddy! I need my Daddy! Where is my Daddy?!" Our hearts broke for him as the adults at home that day moved quietly about the house, keeping busy and trying to hold back their own tears. At times like this it was difficult to keep a good perspective.

Chapter Twelve

$$\sim\!\!\bigwedge\!\!\sim$$

Day 6—Thursday

Some parents said that their children seemed eager to take up the cause of praying for Bruce's toes—or "pink piggies" as they called them. This need seemed to be something they understood. And God heard them too. During the night our friend Jep said he witnessed the flow of blood begin to return, literally watching a visible line of colour move slowly down Bruce's feet and eventually to the very tips of his toes. The news on Facebook that morning: "Pink toes!!!!"

Once again, people would share with me that they didn't really believe that God answered *their* prayers, but when they followed the Facebook posts and prayed for another little thing, and that prayer was answered, and then another...and another...and another...they became excited. I heard so many times, "I know that lots of people are praying at the same time and everything, but for some reason I just really feel like God is answering *my* prayers!" Seeing those prayers answered let them know that God *did* hear them. He *did* respond to them. Their prayers were important. *They* were important.

By that morning, Bruce was nearly off one of his blood pressure medications entirely and on less than half the dose of the other one.

While He Lay Dying

His lower legs and feet felt like they had life in them again. His hands were warm and soft when I held them and more like my husband's hands than those of a corpse. My hopes rose higher.

I was able to eat my first meal without throwing it up! I went back home to my house, which was still bedecked with pink and purple birthday party streamers dangling from the light fixtures. Sagging ribbons trailed behind balloons that levitated a couple of feet off the kitchen floor and looked like some sort of sad sci-fi robots. Keziah had begged her grandmothers not to take the decorations down until Daddy saw them.

The baby had let me sleep most of the night for the first time, and I laughed and played with my kids in the morning. Seeing life in Bruce's body had injected more life into mine. I realized that I had been holding my breath for so long; it was time to take care of myself.

I sat on a rug in the kid's bedroom and played princesses and dinosaurs. We walked to the park, ate grapes and animal cookies and threw sticks off the bridge into sun-dappled Henderson Lake. Little Axel ran ahead shouting, as he often does, "Mommy! Mommy! Watch this! Watch this!" and hopped on one foot or performed a crooked summersault on the newly bare brown grass. Baby Vivia, happy in the stroller, gurgled and cooed and practiced her brand-new beaming smile. I called to Axel who was getting too far ahead. "Look! Mommy, look! Alphabets!" he yelled back.

He bent down and traced large letters spray-painted on the asphalt path. Someone had written the word "FEARLESS" there on the road just before the foot bridge. On the pavement on the other side were the words "LOVE IS LOUDER." Yes. No fear. God's love is louder than the roar of fear. It was so good to have a break for a while.

Back at the hospital, the waiting room had a different air about it as well. The atmosphere was lighter, and people were excited to see what the Lord was going to do next. The waiting room was off a side corridor, tucked away out of view of the busier parts of the rest of the hospital. Thoughtful people brought fruit, homemade cookies and buns, bottles of juice or water and little packets of cheese and sausage for those who stayed to pray for long hours. Someone was always willing to do a Starbucks or Tim Horton's run to bring back coffee and donuts. Musicians often brought their guitars and played worship songs softly in the background. A sheet of paper on the bulletin board on the wall kept track of miracles needed and miracles seen written in black sharpie pen.

People often commented that they came in trepidation, worried about the tension and sadness they expected to encounter, and instead felt a wall of love and peace as they entered this room that had seen so much sorrow in the past. The atmosphere of peace was palpable. I was actually enjoying this little oasis of love. Staff kindly stretched the rules to allow more people than usual to stay, as long as they didn't disturb any patients or their families. Occasionally they even permitted more than the usual two family members short visits in Bruce's room.

Then we found out why. They didn't think we would be there long. They didn't think Bruce would make it.

In fact, I found out that privately the doctors and nurses had given Bruce a *zero percent* chance of survival. Those who were aware of this prognosis avoided talking to me because they didn't want to ruin my faith for big things by giving me such a bad report. Other doctors, nurses, and lab techs later confirmed they had heard the same thing. Afterwards, we heard from some nurses that they had dreaded coming into work each day fearing they would hear the news that Bruce had died.

There in the waiting room, I told a nurse, "Sometimes when I held his stiff cold hand I could tell his body was starting to die…"

She held my hand in hers and with tears in her eyes said, "Oh Lara, he was already mostly dead."

After they finished changing dressings and I was allowed back into his room, feeling his warm hand gave me hope and I could hear things like that better. Although he was certainly improving in some respects, he was still on life support, still critical, still had kidney failure, still had pneumonia, and still had a scary low platelet count. They were transfusing platelets to up his numbers but couldn't risk giving him too much because the risk of clotting was already so high. At that point, his blood was clotting in the dialysis machine, causing it to shut down and forcing them to throw out any blood still in the machine. As a result, he needed many transfusions, and a lot of withdrawals were made at the blood bank on his behalf.

While He Lay Dying

People were still asking how they could help, and our friend Dr. Crawford encouraged those who could to donate blood. The response was so great that those who phoned the blood clinic couldn't get appointments for weeks!

Despite the serious condition Bruce was in, what was encouraging to me was that even with an apparent zero percent chance of survival, there were still signs of improvement happening and God's hand at work. The doctor had even mentioned Bruce was "stable," and though I knew that under the circumstances stable merely meant that there were no new crises at the moment, I grabbed every bit of hope I could. I went home that night feeling lighter and with excitement of what else the Lord would do. I slept well that night.

Chapter Thirteen

Day 7—Dark Friday (Good Friday)

I made a habit of always sleeping with my phone right beside me just in case the hospital called. They never had. I mostly used it to call and get an update every time I was up with the baby. I should say they never had...until now. That morning, on Good Friday, I was startled out of my sleep by the phone ringing. I looked and saw that it was the ICU calling. My heart sank to the floor. *I thought he was improving? Why would they be calling me now?* I had just talked to someone a few hours earlier when I was up with the baby, and he was doing well.

A new internal medicine specialist had taken over Bruce's case as the previous one was now on holidays, and he was calling me. I could tell by the tone of his voice that things were not good. He told me that they were nearly certain that the infection had spread to Bruce's calf and that they were going to try to get him into the OR as soon as possible. He said that in the interest of saving his life it needed to be done right away. Then he hung up and I cried.

I dragged myself into the shower (which, by the way, is the best place to bawl if you need to). I pulled myself together a bit, and when I came out, I found everyone in the house was frantic. They said the hospital called again. I wasn't getting there fast enough! I thought it

While He Lay Dying

would be hours before they could get him into the operating room so I didn't know I was supposed to be rushing. My mom told me that they were now trying to air ambulance him to a bigger city, and they wanted me there as soon as possible. I looked at my twin friends, Robyn and Becky, who were there with me, and we literally *ran* out of the house as fast as possible! My heart was pounding a mile a minute, and I had no idea what I would find when we got there!

The plan was for my mom to dress the kids, take them to a friend's house, and then join Bruce's parents at the hospital. Bruce's brother, Mark, was still at the hospital after spending the night with him, and my dad had arrived before dawn since he went over to pray every day in the early hours of the morning. He kept phoning my mom to ask where I was.

We sped the whole way, and I ran as fast as I could through the hospital and up to the third floor. When I got to the ICU doors, my brother-in-law and father looked horrible. A few friends who had also heard the news were there waiting for me, crying. Nobody had been in to see him; the nurses wanted me to go in first. When I went in, there was a flurry of activity around Bruce. The doctor was on the phone with a bigger hospital while technicians took an ultrasound of Bruce's lungs. He looked sicker than I had ever seen him.

The doctor explained to me that Bruce's lungs had filled with blood and weren't working at all. He was on 100 percent oxygen, and his body was doing nothing to help him breathe.

He was dying.

The room was filled with doctors, nurses, and respiratory techs moving around frantically, and all seemed to be in a panic. I could feel their fear and their sadness. I just stood in shock, and my world stood still for a few minutes. A nurse put her arm around me and asked me if I wanted her to get someone to come and support me. She went and got my friend Robyn, and we just stood holding each other and crying. After awhile Robyn switched out and Becky came in. I have never seen someone so close to death before, and it offended everything in me for it to be my beloved in that state!

They contemplated air lifting him out, but the bigger hospital said they could do little more for him, and the air ambulance felt their equipment could not support his extensive need for oxygen. They talked about getting him into the operating room as soon as possible, but it was quickly determined that he was too unstable to push even 50 feet across the hallway into the OR! Not only that, but the ventilator in the OR didn't go to 100 percent and they wouldn't be able to sustain him in there. The decision was made to call the surgeon in and do surgery right there in his ICU room, something that had only been done one other time in the history of the hospital, and that was only because the OR had been full.

They never told me to "say goodbye," but everything in the air and their body language was screaming it. But I couldn't! I couldn't say goodbye to him. He wasn't supposed to die; it wasn't his time. I just couldn't go there. So, I held his hand and told him that he had to fight.

I cried out to God for mercy and healing, but I couldn't say goodbye!

I later found out that the head nurse had considered moving Bruce to a double room where there was more space, so that they could bring people in by groups to come say their goodbyes. But they didn't because he was so critical that he probably wouldn't survive even that little trip.

I went back out to the waiting room and wept in the arms of my friends for a while. Then I grabbed Bruce's brother and asked him to come in with me. We went together and wept together at the side of his bed. We told Bruce how much he meant to us and held nothing back. We urged him to fight through this! He *had* too! We couldn't lose him! Not now! There had been too many miracles to end this way. This couldn't be the end!

I left Mark alone for a moment to see if Bruce's parents were there yet. While I was gone, Mark said that Bruce started to choke and spit up a lot of blood. Thankfully, the specialist and nurses acted swiftly and skillfully to deal with this catastrophic bleed in his lungs, but it was the most horrible thing he said he had ever seen, and he was so thankful that I had left when I had.

Upon consulting with the other hospital, it was advised they put Bruce into isolation and treat him as if he had influenza as well because they had recently had three patients with a dual diagnosis. So when I went back in with Bruce's parents, his brother, and Bishop

While He Lay Dying

Todd, they had us all wear gowns and masks with face shields and gloves. Bruce's bed was pushed to the far corner of the room in preparation for the impending surgery.

Many people kept telling me how strong I was throughout this. It was never my intention to come across as "strong." I was simply walking out all of the emotions I felt when I felt them. I believe anything that looked like strength was God carrying me, and it was His strength that they were seeing. In this moment, I was so broken. I did the only thing I could think of to do; I curled up in a ball in the fetal position on the floor and put my earphones in my ears, played music to draw me into the Lord and drown out all the "noise." Then I cried my heart out. His parents stood beside me praying and declaring the goodness of the Lord, and Mark and Todd laid hands on him.

It was Good Friday, but it felt more like *Dark Friday*.

I asked the Lord what I was supposed to do in that moment, and His answer came swiftly. He told me I was to "cocoon" in Him. He said he had already raised up an army to fight for Bruce and that my only job was to cocoon in Him. He would take care of me; I just needed to focus on Him and let the prayer warriors do their jobs. Bruce was going to live; I just needed to survive this.

When we left his room for the last time before surgery, Todd looked at me and told me he was still 100 percent sure Bruce was going to live. Sometimes it was hard for me to be so sure of something by faith and yet see something so contrary by sight. But I had to cling to the Spirit. I had to.

While we were waiting in the waiting room for the surgeon to come, Bruce's cousin and his wife Lauren came running in. She took one look at me, ran to me, pulled me into her arms, and began to pray and declare with a passion and fire that I have never seen in her. She was literally yelling, "WE BELIEVE! WE BELIEVE! WE BELIEVE!" I later asked her where that came from, because typically she is a quiet, gentle, laid-back kind of girl. She said she didn't even feel like it was her praying.

Then my mother, after having dropped the kids off at a friend's place, rushed in, breathless. She looked around and saw all the red eyes and stooped shoulders and said, "Kezi says we need a new song!"

A couple of weeks before all this started, Keziah asked for a song to be played repeatedly when we were in the van. She developed such a fondness for the song that she insisted on hearing that song on repeat every time we got in the van—every single day. The song is not a children's song, but "Strings" by Misty Edwards. My mom relayed the conversation they'd had in the van.

"Do you want to hear "Strings" again, Kezi?" she asked.

"Okay," Keziah said.

Then she suddenly changed her mind, "No! Not Strings! Play the next song. The next song is a good song. We need the next song today!"

Axel chimed in, "Play the next song! Play the next song!"

The next song was "I Believe that You're My Healer." Keziah, who had not been told about the crisis, sang along from the back seat, "Nothing is impossible! Nothing is impossible for you, Jesus!"

"Again!" she insisted when the song was finished. She sang along more loudly this time.

By the time my mom dropped the kids off, found a parking spot and rushed up to the ICU waiting room, she knew the Lord had given us all a gift through our little girl.

Nevertheless, the next two hours were literally the longest, hardest, and darkest of my entire life. After the Good Friday service let out, more than a hundred people from the church came to the hospital to pray for Bruce. The waiting room was packed, and the three closest hallways filled with people pacing, praying, crying, and fighting for my husband. People from other churches showed up too. I later heard that the hospital had never seen anything like it before! Even with so many people surrounding us at the hospital, I was told most of my church family stayed behind at the church building to pray for him.

I am typically a huggy, touchy, feely kind of person, but for some reason I didn't want to be hugged by anyone or hear any condolences in my ears. I didn't want to feel or hear the fear that was already so palpable. I did what the Lord said. I tuned everyone and everything out and cocooned in him. I put my earphones on and listened to one song on repeat, over and over and over again. Even though the halls filled with people, it drew me into such a sweet place of intimacy with the Lord.

While He Lay Dying

This is what I listened to:

"Come to Me"
(By Jenn Johnson, John Hendrickson)

I am the Lord your God, I go before you now
I stand beside you, I'm all around you
Though you feel I'm far away, I'm closer than your breath
I am with you, more than you know

I am the Lord your peace, no evil will conquer you
Steady now your heart and mind, come into My rest
Oh, let your faith arise, lift up your weary head
I am with you wherever you go

Come to Me, I'm all you need.
Come to Me, I'm everything
Come to Me, I'm all you need.
Come to Me, I'm your everything

I am your anchor, in the wind and the waves
I am your steadfast, so don't be afraid
Though your heart and flesh may fail you, I'm your faithful strength
I am with you wherever you go

Come to Me, I'm all you need.
Come to Me, I'm your everything
Come to Me, I'm all you need.
Come to Me, I'm your everything

Don't look to the right or to the left but keep your eyes on Me
You will not be shaken, you will not be moved ooh
I am the hand to hold, I am the truth, I am the way
Just come to Me, come to Me, cause I'm all that you need. *

Each time I made my lap by the doors of the ICU and I could see nurses, doctors and trays and machines and everything through the windows, I felt scared, but then the song would inevitably get to the part where it says, "Don't look to the right or to the left but keep your eyes on Me."

I stopped looking in the windows, stopped making eye contact with sad people, but rather walked with my head up and pictured the face of Jesus with every step I took. I think I actually listened to that song 56 times over that whole day. But the Lord cocooned me, cared for me, poured faith into me, spoke to me, and carried me!

I posted these words that morning during his surgery:

> *I have been to healing revivals and seen one man pray and thousands healed. Today as my husband is in surgery in his room clinging and fighting for life, I witness thousands of people praying for one man! There is a unified army here and around the world praying for Bruce because we all know his healing means so much more for the Body of Christ and for healing in this country. The halls are packed, the waiting room's packed...And together we fight and declare that Bruce will live! God is in control!! Fight with us. Even if you feel you don't know how to pray. Just cry out to God.*

Chapter Fourteen

As I was walking past the ICU doors again, trying to keep my focus, all of a sudden they swung wide open, leaving me standing there frozen, staring in like a little child. One of the nurses looked at me standing there and smiled. She then gave me two thumbs up, and I let my breath out for the first time in hours and fell into the arms of a friend nearby.

A few minutes later, another nurse came out to the main hallway. Scanning the crowd, she found me and beckoned me to come. I followed her and on the way grabbed Bruce's mom and dad.

"His surgery went really well," she said. "The surgeon found more infected tissue on his thigh, a little more near his previous incision, and removed most of the skin and fascia on his calf. Thankfully, they did not have to remove any muscle. He is more stable now. His lungs are responding a bit better, and we are going to move him to a new, bigger room."

She put her arms around my shoulders. I smiled through my tears and thanked her.

I later heard that the surgeon that was on call was the right person to have there because he had been a war surgeon with Doctors Without Borders doing all kinds of surgeries in crazier situations than in an ICU room. This didn't even faze him!

While He Lay Dying

We shared the news with everyone in the hallway, and there was a ton of cheering! Then the waiting room erupted with singing, "The enemy has been defeated! We have the victory!"

I was able to see him shortly after that, and the atmosphere in the room was so much different. Somehow, I knew we had just won the greatest of battles. I felt so much peace about how he was doing that I was able to go home and fall into my bed from total exhaustion.

When I went back later that night, they said that he continued to improve slowly as the day went on. I spoke to the specialist who told me then that Bruce was by far and wide, without any comparison, the sickest person in the sickest ward in the entire hospital and had been for quite some time. I later found out that at least one other person in the ICU, who wasn't as sick as Bruce, had unfortunately passed away that same day. I was saddened to hear that, and it really drove home to me just how much of a miracle it was that Bruce lived through that day!

Day 8—Saturday

Facebook update:

> It's amazing how important words are to me these days. "Improvement" was my first favourite, then "stable" and yesterday the word "ALIVE" never had so much meaning to me.
>
> I can't even express all the emotions that were going through me while they were operating in his room. But the Lord told me to just cocoon in Him and think only of Jesus. He truly carried me through the most difficult two hours of my entire life.
>
> Today Bruce is once again stable. His blood pressure is steadily improving and they have gotten him completely off one of his drugs (hooooray!). His platelet count went up but he still bled out of his wound significantly today so they are giving him five units of blood. His lungs have significantly less blood in them, and he is on 50% respirator (it was 100% yesterday). He is on 12 IVs, and his room is filled with machines, and we are now wearing gowns and masks with splash shields and gloves to visit him. It's like some B-rated sci-fi movie (he would be proud).

So, we are seeing some improvements and yet there are some things getting worse. Please join us to pray specifically for his blood, the healing of his wound (and that no more infection would come back), and his lungs. Oh, and no more surprises.

Thank you all for your love! I am especially humbled that so many people would pray so diligently for him for a long haul and not just one or two days. This battle won't be won in a day, but I am confident that we will win.

At this point, I was more than done with this. It had been a week in the "valley of the shadow of death," and I just wanted my husband back! I knew that one day he would be making me laugh again, but this journey was so ugly, so horrible, and so very long! I can't describe the faith I had throughout this, other than that it must have come from the Lord, because everything I saw or heard from the medical staff was very contrary to what I, and many others were hearing in our spirits.

It was also really encouraging to have the kind of amazing family and friends Bruce and I have surrounding us with their faith and prayers and practical help—what a boost. Some of my close girl friends, Becky, Robyn, and Micheline, even travelled to help me and care for my children, sacrificing their time and their normal lives to lift us up. Everyone was just an unbelievable support, both on the home front and at the hospital.

After Bruce went into isolation for possible influenza, the hospital staff told us they had to limit who could go in the room due to fear of spreading infection. They said only Bruce's immediate family and myself would be allowed. Bruce's mom, a strong and beautiful woman of God said, "Bishop Todd needs to be in here as well." She went to bat to have him included. Somehow, we all knew that we needed him at Bruce's side! He had the experience of years of learning to rely on more than his own resources. He knew how to lean on God for wisdom in fighting battles like this, which was more than just a physical battle. This was also a spiritual battle. I knew that when Bruce woke up he would be looking for Todd. Bruce's mother was so convinced of our need for Todd at his side she was willing to give up her own spot to make it happen! Now that is sacrifice! Thankfully, they didn't make her do that and kindly allowed

While He Lay Dying

Todd to be considered immediate family. I am forever grateful for her willingness to fight for something that was so important to all of us.

Because of the new restrictions, many of the pastors, friends and extended family who had been praying all day and all night for him in the past were no longer allowed to be in the room with him. You might think that they would then disband and go home. But they didn't. They just took to the halls and the waiting room and prayed all night there.

Bruce's close friends Stephen Barbour and Amos Martel were not only my comic relief but they both had fierce faith for Bruce's miracle. Stephen, a big man with a tender heart, frequently stood at the far door to the ICU, hands tucked in his hoodie pockets, peering through the windows where he could see the entrance to Bruce's room. He was so convinced that Bruce would get out of that bed that he didn't want to miss it when it happened. Every time the nurses rushed into Bruce's room, Stephen would wonder if it was happening and jumped up excitedly! He waited at that window day and night ready for Bruce to wake up and get out of that chrome-railed bed. I would be sitting in Bruce's room by his bedside, and when I looked up, I could see a blond bearded face peeking through the window down at the end of the hall waiting for the miracle. That is faith, my friends! It is that kind of faith that stirred mine to greater heights. The following day was Easter. Sounds like a good day to wake up, doesn't it?

Chapter Fifteen

Day 9—Resurrection Sunday (Easter)

I put on Bruce's favourite dress. It's a Latin red wrap-around dress with fabric roses circling the neckline that he picked out for me in Mexico on our previous anniversary trip. I got all dolled up and zipped to the hospital before church started. Bishop Todd was already in the room when I arrived. I cannot even begin to describe the electric, excited feelings I had rushing through my body. Today was Resurrection Sunday; he had to wake up! I was full of faith and anticipation. Todd laughed when I told him I was wearing make-up and Bruce's favourite dress and then proceeded to cover it all up with a face shield and big yellow gown! It's the thought that counts, right?

We spent the next half hour trying to convince Bruce to wake up! Todd enticed him with, "If you wake up now I'll let you preach the Easter service!"

At one point we both said in unison, "BRUCE! It's Resurrection Sunday! Time to wake up!!"

And he opened his eye!

It was just one eye, for one brief moment, but Todd and I were hooting and hollering like a bunch of cheerleaders!

While He Lay Dying

When I went to the hospital that morning, I expected him to get up out of his bed and walk out of his room. I dreamed the night before that his wounds were completely healed. In the dream Bruce stood up and started pulling out all the tubes and ripping off the bandages. He even came with us to church. I fully believed it could, and even would happen.

One thing I have learned on my faith journey is that there is no harm in having big dreams and not having them come true. Sometimes we are so afraid of disappointment that we stop dreaming. I can tell you this, though, that without dreaming, *everything* in our lives is disappointing! I have learned to step out in faith and get my hopes up. Lots of times I am wrong, and I simply shake it off and thank God for His plan and move on to the next thing to hope for. I believe that it is because I never stop hoping or dreaming big that I have been able to see so many big dreams come true.

Don't let disappointments in your life squelch your ability to dream in the Lord. He is a good God, and if you get it wrong, just trust that He has something better in store for you. Push yourself to dream again. That's what a life of faith looks like. I imagine that one day I will get better at hearing His voice and that as I become more intimate with Him, my heart will align more with His, and my wants will be His wants through me. I'll get it right more than I get it wrong. Until then, I will step out, fall sometimes, get back up, and do it again. And occasionally I will have it right and have amazing stories to tell!

If your faith is small, then just be faithful with what you have. Step out just beyond your comfort zone and see what happens. This is how we build faith—through stepping out and experiencing God come through. This verse has been a motto for me for years, every time I feel like I am not strong in any area, whether it is in talents or spiritual gifts or faith or love or responsibilities:

"His master replied, 'Well done, good and faithful servant! You have been faithful with a few things; I will put you in charge of many things. Come and share your master's happiness!'" (Matthew 25:21).

I want to be faithful even with the smallest amount of things so that one day He will help me to be faithful with many (big) things! So, even when my faith is small, I will step out to the degree in which I can and be faithful with it.

Bishop Todd and I went to the Easter Sunday service at church after Bruce opened his one eye. When Todd told the congregation what had happened, they erupted with a shout! There wasn't a dry eye in the place! Everyone stood and cheered for a long time. We weren't cheering because Bruce did such a good job of opening his eye; we were cheering because there is so much power in the resurrection of Jesus Christ, and they knew it is *that* resurrection power that was going to heal my husband completely. This was just a foretaste of what was to come!

Chapter Sixteen

Days 10–11

Although Bruce was still the sickest person in the hospital, the doctor said he was amazed at his progress. He was "leaps and bounds" better than he had been just days before. He was stable, and the improvements were slow but coming. We continued to post miracles we were praying for on the board in the waiting room, and at this point, the next most important need was his blood condition. We needed to see those platelets up! He was bleeding out of his wound daily, having many transfusions, and still at a high risk of serious clotting.

However, I was encouraged that he was off the blood pressure meds completely and was even slowly becoming aware of our voices. When I called his name, he scrunched his eyes. I loved seeing him respond, even a little bit. It felt so amazing to know he was in there! I spent the whole day in his room, reading him encouraging portions of scripture. I laid my iPhone on his chest, between the tubes and wires, and played worship music for him. I held it up to his ear and played videos of our children. When I played a video of our eldest saying, "Hi Daddy! I miss you," his eyebrows rose up. It is amazing how expressive eyebrows can be when that is all you can move!

While He Lay Dying

The doctors and nurses all seemed surprised that Bruce was doing so well at this point! We finally got the test results for the influenza virus back. He tested negative, which was a great relief, especially since it meant that we could take off the hot stuffy space suits!

Sometimes during the long waits when staff performed procedures and I was shooed out of the room because they needed the space, I would find myself talking to whoever was in the waiting room praying for him. The afternoons were often quiet with just one or two praying in there. I started getting into the habit of asking them what the Lord was showing them. It was always encouraging to me to know that this was bigger than Bruce and our little family. Many times I learned God was touching people in similar ways. A lot of people had known the pain of seeing loved ones die in the past. Some felt their prayers hadn't been answered in those times, and our situation was bringing up a lot of painful memories and questions for them. The beautiful thing was that they were there praying for Bruce because they sincerely wanted to heal in those areas themselves. Many of them found that partnering in Bruce's miracle brought peace to places in their heart where grief and disappointment still lingered.

Two of our dear friends Jody and Jaci were at the hospital day in and day out. I swear that nearly every time I went into the waiting room, at least one of them was there. I kept whispering to Jody's sister-in-law that he didn't need to be there. You see, Jody and Jaci lost their beautiful little girl not long ago. It was in an ICU unit just like this that they said goodbye to their precious daughter. I couldn't even fathom how hard this must have been for them. I am sure that some of you reading this can identify with them. Here is their story:

Jody:

> *Night after night at the hospital, we experienced joy and the presence of God among believers, in the worst of circumstances. There was an undeniable presence of God and for me especially on Good Friday, Bruce's worst day. My brother and I both felt an urgent need to leave near the beginning of the morning service at River of Life church and to get to the hospital as soon as we could. When we arrived at the ICU, I could feel God's power flood over me as I knelt and began to pray.*

There was an overwhelming sense of peace and the anointing of the Holy Spirit as I prayed. From what we understood, things were very grim for Bruce that morning; however, there were close to a hundred people from our church praying all around the ICU. A few hours later that morning we received the good news that his surgery went well and he was stable.

Nearly seven years ago on July 24, 2006 we experienced a horrible tragedy: our two-and-a-half-year-old daughter died in a sudden choking accident. Although she lived two days in the hospital and we prayed fervently, we did not receive her healing and she passed into the Lord's presence. I began to understand what it meant to be "struck down but not destroyed" (2 Corinthians 4:9). I am not a crier, but I cried nearly every day for a year. My wife and I were truly rocked to the core.

We did not receive the miracle we had hoped for, but we did see other miracles as a result of this event—a strengthened marriage, closer intimacy with God, and a miraculous physical sign of comfort the night before her burial. These are just a few of the miracles that God performed around this horrible tragedy. Probably the greatest outcomes, though, were the salvations in people around us as we felt an urgency to share the gospel with people because of our increased sense of reality of the eternal. There's no greater miracle than salvation, a life changed for eternity.

The one thing that amazed me the most was the support we received from the body of Christ during our ordeal. I have never felt so loved in all my life by family, friends, pastors, and people we didn't even know. That definitely played a huge part in our healing. I can truly say that today I stand healed of this tragedy, no longer burdened by it because of what Jesus has healed in me and healed in our family. Even so, Emma is deeply missed, loved, and forever cherished, and one day, my hope will be realized as I see her and my Lord face to face.

This tragedy did not hinder my thoughts that God is loving and that God wanted to, and very much could, heal Bruce. My motivation was purely that I loved Bruce and couldn't imagine life without him. I am glad that I responded with the same love that people poured out on us, but it wasn't that I was trying to return that love in kind. The love for Bruce came out of my heart and it could not be contained even for an instant. Thank You, Lord, for working Your love in all of us.

While praying for Bruce, one thing I experienced, which I have never before to the same degree, was the ease of raising the shield of faith to doubt, even in the harsh physical realities that he was facing. One scripture that really stood out to me during Bruce's ordeal was Mark 11:24, "Therefore I say to you, all things for which you pray and ask, believe that you have received them, and they will be granted you" (NASB). The Lord raised up faith in us, and when we all walked in that faith, we received Bruce's miracle, praise the name of Jesus.

People often ask, "Why do bad things happen to good people?" I don't know. Factually, I know that we live in a fallen world because of our sin, and this has brought consequences. Why God doesn't heal in certain circumstances? I don't know. God knows, and I do love Him and trust that He always has our best in mind because He loves us more that we could ever imagine. He demonstrated this by His death on the cross for our sins. Although we did not receive healing for our daughter in this life, we will see her perfect healing in the next. That is our hope, and one day it will be realized. Amen.

Days 12–15

As usual, the first thing I did in the morning was call the ICU to get an update on the night before.

"Has no one called you yet?" the nurse asked.

Umm okay, not good words to start a conversation with. It turns out Bruce was running a fever of 40.4 Celsius (105 Fahrenheit). Fevers in patients in his condition indicate the body is fighting something, usually infection. So, off he went to another CT scan. Moving a person on life support requires the logistical skills of a major army manoeuvre and was not undertaken lightly. It took several staff members a good part of the day to do this. He was attached to a respirator, a dialysis machine, oxygen, heart, and blood pressure monitors, all manner of tubes, and 12 IV bags on poles! His incisions were still open, and he still weighed three hundred and thirty pounds!

"The doctors are concerned that the infection has perhaps moved into his abdomen or trunk area. That wouldn't be good. There is also the possibility of a fungal infection as well. They just want to rule out those possibilities."

"More infection?"

"And...while he's down there, they want to check and make sure he hasn't bled out in his brain as well."

I blinked as the tears slipped down my cheek. I held the baby tighter out of fear of dropping her, and croaked out the words, "His brain?"

So, once again I rushed down to the hospital to sit and wait on results. Waiting is something I learned to do. I had stood many times by the closed blank wooden door. Beside the door to the ICU was an intercom with a red button and a sign taped beside it that read, "Please push button before entering." I learned to wait for someone to answer the intercom to be let into the ICU. I learned to wait while they checked with his nurses to see if anyone was allowed in his room. If they were changing his dressings, the wait could be a long one. I learned to wait for specialists to come onto the unit and give me updates. I learned to wait while tests were being done. I learned to wait on the Lord.

The result of the scans was "normal." They gave no indication of where the infection might be.

We were approaching the weekend, and a new surgeon had just come on. I came into the room, and the medical team was deliberating about what to do. Because Bruce's whole body had swollen up over a hundred pounds more than usual, that meant everything was swollen. His right leg, however, was red and very swollen, and they began discussing whether they should cut into it to see if that's where the infection was. It sounded like a done deal, so I went out to the waiting room to wait some more.

When the nurse came back out, he said they had changed their minds. The surgeon had been on the phone with the Infectious Disease specialist asking their advice, and because Bruce's whole body was swollen there wasn't clear enough evidence to warrant cutting open another leg and needlessly risking more infection. So they were going to wait another day.

The next day his right leg didn't look as red as it did before and the doctors decided that the infection was likely not in that leg. (Thank

While He Lay Dying

You, Jesus!) So, they started looking at the left leg again. They kept saying that it looked good but that it was one of the only options left to consider as far as the fever was concerned.

We asked everyone to pray for his legs and for the fever to break. I began to realize that all along we had been targeting all kinds of symptoms to get better, and we were seeing progress and miracles in those areas, but we weren't fighting the enemy and stopping him in his tracks! We weren't praying to stop the infection itself! I sent out an urgent prayer request to pray that this attack would stop!

A little later, I received this email from an old friend:

> *Just another little note to say that I'm praying for you and Bruce and a little story about that: I was woken up out of my sleep twice this weekend and reminded to pray for Bruce's recovery! I woke up with really bad leg cramps in my calf muscles on Friday night (more intense on the right leg)...which I've never had before...and, still being really sleepy, I was a bit frustrated that they hurt and I couldn't get rid of them right away. My first sleepy thought though was, "Wow, I should pray for Bruce."...And a few minutes after praying, the leg cramps stopped and I fell back asleep. Same thing happened the next night (Saturday) but not as long or as strong and more intense on the left calf.*
>
> *God is reminding people to pray for Bruce (and you) at all hours and through pretty creative means!*
>
> *Love you lots!*
>
> *Kathleen*

I love how God works and how he speaks to people in such neat ways! Bruce had learned in the past that sometimes the Lord pointed out another person's pain by letting him feel it himself. At first, it was confusing until he learned to inquire if anyone around him was experiencing that sort of pain and if so, he would quietly go pray for him or her. He has seen people miraculously healed this way. However, this friend didn't even know that about Bruce, nor had these kinds of things happened to her before. I just love that God spoke to someone in the depths of night, in the same way He commonly speaks to Bruce, on a night when prayer for his right calf was desperately needed, and then again on the next night when prayer for his left calf was needed. She knew nothing of the doctors thinking the right leg was also infected.

I understand that when these stories come out and people have their own terms and lingo to describe them, we can get our walls up out of fear. All sorts of hurts and confused emotions can result. My favourite thing about God is that He doesn't need someone who has seen this before or has experience with it. All He needs is someone willing to pay attention to what He might be communicating to him or her and to be faithful in following His leading. People, it is not about denominations here! It is about God being God and the Holy Spirit awakening people in His gentle way and in His perfect timing! I am so thankful for this woman's faithfulness to listen to the Lord through such "creative means." I believe her experience was actually an answer to everyone's prayers and instrumental in the healing of Bruce's right calf!

Chapter Seventeen

Days 15–18

The fever broke! In fact, they never found the source of it. It simply went back to normal. I was glad to see it go; that marked the end of the attack for me. Now it was all about him getting better and getting out of the woods for good!

His platelet count was on the rise, and his blood condition was becoming less of a concern. His kidneys were getting better, and his creatinine levels hovered in the 300s (which is a nice drop from the 534 they were at originally!) but they still had a long way to go before they were functioning normally.

He was gradually becoming more responsive as the nurses slowly dialed back the sedation to see what he could handle. One day, I said in his ear, "Bruce, it's Lara. Open your eyes, honey!" And he did!

But, oh my, I wasn't ready for what I saw.

Not only could he not focus, but one of his eyes was wonky. I have seen lazy eyes before, and this is not what I am talking about. I am talking about a "crazy eye," or so I called it. When he opened his eyes, you could see that he had no control over his right eye. It was pointing down and sitting over in the far right corner of his socket all by itself. Honestly, it freaked me out a bit. I wasn't expecting that at all!

A million thoughts ran through my mind as I encouraged him to close them again.

I left his room right after that to find his doctor and ask if that was normal for the eyes after so long under sedation.

"No, Lara, it's not," he said. "That's why I called for the brain scan."

He was worried about bleeding in the brain due to the low platelets, which would indicate there was brain damage. Thankfully, the scan showed his brain was okay. The doctor wasn't able to tell me what the cause was or whether it was permanent, so a text went out to Bruce's closest friends to keep his eye in their prayers. Bruce makes his living teaching over the internet, using his computer all day long. The thought of him not having use of that eye or not being able to think as well was devastating to contemplate. Besides, I just felt like he was to come out of this and make a 100% recovery, and that just didn't fit, so it was time to pull up the faith boots and hope, not in what I could see, but what I could not yet see! I needed an upgrade in my vision as well.

I said earlier that Bruce is a teacher through and through, and it is amazing that even in his sleep he was still teaching people. A friend of ours found this post Bruce wrote a couple of years earlier for the church blog. People all over were now reading his blog about trials. Who knew it was just what we would need when his body was suffering.

March 9, 2011 (Written by Bruce, two years earlier)

When the book of James mentions the phrase "trials of many kinds" in chapter 1, I find it comforting that God has given a fairly broad definition of what a trial is. Whether it's an unexpected tragedy, marital strife, unemployment, persecution, a wayward child, a wilderness season, etc., these circumstances are usually felt as trials, and God lovingly acknowledges that. But what's even more interesting to me is how the trial actually progresses and eventually ends. Often, the aspect of it feeling like a trial ends sooner than the circumstances that initially produced those feelings. And it's something I'd like to explore a bit further here.

My first trial came fairly late, in my early 20s. Up to then, I had lived quite a sheltered life: I had super parents who loved the Lord, a great church and spiritual community around me, and a grace from the Lord of real hunger and desire for Him, coupled with a constantly accessible sense of His presence. Life had been cushy—no major setbacks, traumas, or issues, and when preachers would speak of trials, I really couldn't relate.

But then, in the last year of my undergraduate degree in science, around Christmas time, I became aware that I knew a trial was coming. I can't explain how I knew—I just knew that I knew that a trial was coming and that I should prepare...somehow (since what the nature of this trial would be was unknown to me). And so, next September approached and I was off to a different city to do my teaching degree, and within days of my arrival, suddenly, without warning, all sense of God's presence and initiative in my life was gone. God seemed absent, the fire of hunger and passion seemed gone, and I found myself wondering how I had sinned, or how I had offended God that He would so acutely leave me. I distinctly remember kneeling down beside my bed to pray, only to flop my hands and head on the bed in despair, wondering what I would do now in my prayer times since God had decided not to join me in them. And worship—well, worship was...connectionless. I would worship and feel nothing of God's presence, no activity in my spirit, it seemed, and remain mostly emotionless, while others around me would weep, with hands raised, as God's Spirit would quite obviously move upon everyone, it seemed, as they worshipped. Weeks turned into months, which turned into years, and I wondered when and if I'd ever sense God's presence again.

Eventually however, like a captured animal that finally acknowledges its fate, I learned to cope, and I learned valuable secrets throughout the experience, which lasted about ten years. I remember coming to the realization that I had been worshipping God because of how great His presence felt when we worshipped, as opposed to how great He simply was. I learned to walk by faith, and not by feelings—and that's because I had to! I learned that my seeming super-spirituality was not a result of my awesomeness and great choices but rather His divine grace to me flowing through me. I developed a deep mercy in my heart toward others who were struggling with sin as I saw the depths of my depravity apart from Him.

While He Lay Dying

But the interesting thing is that eventually, it was not a trial any-more. Perhaps like how a person that becomes blind develops super-sensitivity in his or her other senses and begins to love them, I began to love the depth that it was creating in me. The deeper the pain of His absence, the deeper I appreciated what it was producing in me.

Looking back, I actually don't think I did all that well in the sea-son by some accounts. But it's funny how God can still use our imper-fections and weakness to accomplish some of His greatest things! For example, my church volunteering took a back seat for a while as I ques-tioned my prior motives, while God used this opportunity to begin to fix my broken identity. Specifically, in my extreme letting go of striving, He was more able to show me that He still loved me as a son, regardless of how much I performed as a servant.

At some point in this wilderness season, I actually began to like it somewhat. I was learning to commune with God better in terms of hear-ing His voice, I was receiving great revelation from the Word, and I was learning to perceive His hand in everyday life. And occasionally, I would even have gentle glimpses of His presence here and there, though never for long, and in general, I felt like I was maturing and becoming more bal-anced. And I liked that effect. Looking back, I think I no longer consid-ered it a trial as such but rather simply life as I now knew it.

It's interesting to note that my circumstances hadn't really changed. Other than the occasional flash of His presence, God was still very "absent." (However, one could say that God was in fact present, and I was merely learning to perceive His presence differently.) But something had obviously changed since it wasn't really feeling like a trial anymore. And the thing I feel that changed the most was simply this: my perspec-tive. In short, I was adopting more and more of a heavenly perspective (God's view of things) regarding my circumstances, and it was bringing about a greater peace. My faith was growing.

There's a Bible story that powerfully illustrates the difference between a heavenly perspective and an earthly one. Remember how Elisha and his servant were entirely surrounded by the Syrian army? (2 Kings 6) The ser-vant had an accurate earthly perspective: they were surrounded by an entire army bent on one thing—killing them! True. And Elisha also had an accurate perspective, but his was heavenly: surrounding the Syrian army was another army, the Lord's! The servant was terrified yet Elisha was calm. (Remember the disciples in the stormy weather and Jesus asleep?!) For the servant, this was a trial of massive proportions! But for Elisha, I suspect this was no trial at all. Identical circumstance, entirely different state of mind. The difference: heavenly perspective. And note that Elisha's prayer was not for God to give His servant peace or to help him through this trial or to let him feel His presence...It was "God, open his eyes." (In other words, "God, give him a heavenly perspective.")

This lines up exactly with what James writes in regards to trials. First, he says there's such a point you can reach where you actually "count it pure joy"! Why? Because you realize that this trial is actually working toward accomplishing your completion and perfection, getting you to the place where you lack nothing (James 1:4)—accomplishing the very goal of our salvation: making us like Jesus. Second, notice that James' major suggestion in regards to trials is this: if you lack wisdom, ask God for it! Ask Him to give you God's take on this trial—what is God working in you? What is He forging in you? What lack is He removing? In other words, James is saying, ask God for heavenly perspective. Other than that, James merely recommends that after you have heavenly perspective that allows you to see what God is producing in you, don't be impatient as He does it. (Your "trial" may take some time because you're taking some time for God to change!)

In retrospect, my perspective in my own trial was more earthly than heavenly, I'd say. And that's probably why it was a prolonged season that lasted for nearly 11 years by my calculations. I wish I'd taken the Lord's advice to "get ready" for it when He told me it was coming, and now I think I'd know what I'd do. I'd probably have done three things, as James describes. First, I'd have asked for wisdom. ("Does anyone lack wisdom, let Him ask God.") I'd have continually asked God to give me a heavenly perspective to first of all know if this is me, the devil, or God. If it was me, then I'd realize it's my fault and I simply need to change (see James 1:13-17). If it's the devil, then I can trust in the spiritual armour God's given me (Ephesians 6:10-18) and His body around me. And if it's God, then I can ask for more wisdom to know what He's doing and what He's trying to teach me. Second, I'd have practiced habitual thanksgiving and worship ("count it all joy"). Thanksgiving and worship seem to be able to give us heavenly perspective and even the power to break chains (read the rest of the story in Acts 16 surrounding Paul and Silas in prison). And finally, I'd have consciously worked on my patience and not tried to short-circuit God's dealings with me so that I could be perfected in an area ("let patience have its full effect"). And of course, all of the above requires lots of wisdom, so I'd still be asking for lots of that.

In conclusion, I wonder if we can't actually prepare for trials in advance. Can we prepare our hearts to that extent so that when the next trial comes, and it will ("when you face trials of many kinds"), we can fare much better than merely survivors but as actual overcomers? After all, if we can train and prepare ourselves for many other things in life, such as having kids or a new job or good study habits, why can't we prepare ourselves for trials? And if we can (and I think we can, at least in our perspective), perhaps we might find ourselves going through the next trial with more peace and more joy....

Bruce was always good at changing my perspective. He would say to me, "Yes, that is the reality of what is going on, but Lara, what is the greater reality?"

Sometimes we are so much like Elisha's servant, panicking when we see the earthly (and very real) reality. As I was sitting by Bruce's bed, reading his words on trials, finding the faith to believe that his eye would be fine, I asked the Lord, "Can You show me the heavenly reality of this situation?"

I so wanted to open my eyes and see a mountain full of angels, like Elisha and his servant saw. That's when it hit me. He had been showing me that all along! Right at the beginning of this crisis, I had the vision of the angels and Jesus in Bruce's room, and at least ten other people had confirmed that as well! *Oh Lord, forgive me for how easily I forget Your goodness sometimes!* His room was still filled with angels and the presence of God, and no matter how messy things got down here on earth, I could know that God had bigger plans and a bigger army fighting in the spirit realm.

I don't know what your trials are as you are reading this, but I encourage you to ask God for a heavenly perspective of what is going on. It could change everything!

Chapter Eighteen

Day 19—Sedation Vacation

The nurses phoned and said they were tapering down the sedation to see how he would react; if he reacted well, they would keep him off. Again, I rushed to the hospital, but this time with joy in my heart instead of heaviness! Bruce was going to wake up! I felt like this was the day everything truly started moving forward!

Pastor Jep was with me that morning when Bruce woke up. We told Bruce what had happened and that he had been asleep for nearly three weeks! He looked totally shocked! He was still on the respirator so he couldn't talk, although he desperately wanted to! The funny thing is that because the sedation medication affects the memory, it actually took a few more days for Bruce to fully wake up—so we got to tell him what happened for three days in a row, and the look of shock on his face just got funnier and funnier every time!

They had done a tracheostomy a few days prior to taking him off the sedation, putting the tubes directly into a hole cut in his throat, so he had to mouth his words—words totally unrecognizable to us. It was frustrating for him! He tried to write, but he had double vision due to the "crazy eye." After being asleep for three weeks, his muscles had atrophied and his coordination was way off. It was a frustrating but exciting time—frustrating for him, exciting for us. The rest of us were so happy! These problems seemed trivial compared to the life and death battle we faced earlier. His blood work was steadily improving; his healing wounds looked "*Amazing,*" as every nurse gushed; his blood pressure was fantastic. It felt like all we had left to pray for were his lungs, his kidneys, and the wonky eye.

We were given more than one opinion about his kidneys from medical personnel. Some said that with dialysis a few times a week, his kidneys would likely regain function in about three to six months. Some also said we could expect it to take a year. Others said we needed to prepare ourselves for him being on dialysis for the rest of his life, depending on how they responded. Because this seemed like the condition that might take the longest to heal, I decided to post and get everyone praying that Bruce would be able to breathe on his own, as that seemed the most pressing need. We would target the kidney problem later.

The doctors speculated that it would be about five days until we could try getting him off the ventilator. The next day I received a call that they were going to try and plug the plastic tube sticking out of a hole in the base of his throat for a few seconds to see if he might be able to talk.

The nurse told him this could possibly be his only chance to speak for a while. I looked at him straight in the left eye and said, "Make it good, honey!" then leaned in to listen carefully.

He thought long and hard, nodded to them when he was ready and said in a perfect raspy, airy voice, "Luuuuuke, I am your faaaather!" (Or we thought that's what he said. It was kind of hard to hear. He told us later he actually said, "Axel, I am your father," but either way it was great!) Mom and I and the nurses erupted with laughter! We knew he was back!

One of the first things he was able to communicate somehow was that he wanted to see his kids. I had permission to bring them in one at a time as long as I held them and they didn't touch anything. The room was still filled with tubes, cords, and lots of beeping machines, and since his wounds were still open and nurses still monitored him closely, as well as tending to IVs and feeding and other tubes, it was not exactly a child-friendly environment.

As soon as we were given permission, I called my mother and told her to hold off on their baths.

"Bring them to the hospital right away! Daddy is awake and wants to see them!" I told her.

They came as quickly as they could. Keziah dressed herself in a joyful outfit that included a multi-coloured striped sweater, pink tutu, and flowered rain boots. Axel wore a shirt that had samples of the day's menu items on it, and baby Vivia was in cuddly white sleepers, ready for snuggling.

"We're here, Daddy!" Kezi hollered in the atrium when they came through the hospital's main doors.

"We're here! We're here!" Axel echoed, running after her.

"Shh! Some people are sleeping," their Nana cautioned.

"But Daddy's awake!" Axel announced.

I took the children aside, one at a time, to explain to them that Daddy couldn't talk yet. (We covered the trach with a cloth.) I warned them about what they would see and gave instructions that they couldn't touch anything. They didn't seem shocked, although I'm not sure if they knew what to make of their weak, bedridden Daddy, but they were content. Bruce was utterly exhausted, yet thrilled to see them. Uncharacteristically Kezi asked only a few questions, "What's that for? Does his bed move up and down? Can I see your owie, Daddy?" At the very least, I think they came away with a better understanding of why Daddy couldn't come home yet.

On the next visit, Bruce found it easier to stay more alert. The baby was nearly a month older by the time he saw her, and new babies can change a lot in that length of time. He was so weak that he couldn't physically support her sitting up on him. But it was wonderful anyway, and we shared a lot of tears as a family and even more as a couple that week.

Over the next few days, staff detached the ventilator for short periods to let him try to breathe on his own. Bruce's determination showed up, and with the effort of an athlete in training, he focused on taking a breath and letting it out, then taking another breath and another and another until he was exhausted. Then a respiratory technician hooked him up to the machine again. We prayed hard, and he worked hard, and within three days he was completely off the ventilator!

Not long after he woke up, Bruce's blood clogged the filter on the dialysis machine again (which it did pretty much daily), so the kidney specialist said to leave it off for a day and see how he did. When he continued to slowly improve, they left it off for another day. Again, he continued to improve and finally (with the help of a diuretic) started peeing on his own! Because he was doing so well, the specialist decided to take Bruce off dialysis for good! What?! We were expecting dialysis for six months or so at least, and in a few days he was already off? His levels were now in the 200 range and quickly dropping! The specialist said it was remarkable to watch the speed at which the kidneys were recovering!

Fewer people were in the waiting room now. We so appreciated the hospital's staff's generosity to us, especially when so many people showed up, but we understood the need for them to have more order back, so our friends took the goodies and drinks home and now only a couple of people at a time stayed to pray. I arrived one morning and sat on a nubby and slightly grubby upholstered brown chair beside two faithful members of our church who had signed up on the page posted on the cork bulletin board. I noticed a quote someone had printed out and tacked up on the board as well. I don't know how long it had been there. It read:

> *When the devil sees a man or a woman who really believes in prayer, who knows how to pray, and who really does pray, and, above all, when he sees a whole church on its face in prayer, he trembles as much as ever he did—for he knows that his day in that church or community is at an end.* (R.A. Torrey)

But it wasn't just our local church who prayed; many others in the greater big-C Church all across the country and around the world had been praying.

Later I received this message:

> *Lara, my name is Elaine and I am a friend of your aunt and uncle who I first learned your journey through. I learned about Bruce the day I was leaving for Zambia, Africa to work on a project there.*
>
> *One of the things I did there was host a ladies event and over 100 ladies came. I shared very early in the morning your story and how even though I didn't know these people, they were on my heart. My African ladies started to pray...if you have never heard African women pray, it's*

amazing. The roar of sound throughout the thatched roof church stirred each woman's soul.

Those ladies have taken turns praying 24/7—even now, I am in the London airport on my way home, but my ladies are praying in Zambia and will continue until I let the pastor know by text message that all is well. These ladies are 10,000 km away from you, but they/I love you...and will continue to pray.

I was able to find a picture of Bruce and you on your Facebook page, so I printed it and left it with the pastor. Thank you for sharing this journey with us—I know you must be exhausted, but the testimony is going to be amazing....be blessed!

Bruce was awake and starting to communicate. His family and friends were all so happy we could have celebrated and praised God 24 hours a day—if we had not been so exhausted. Laughing, joyous friends lined up for permission to visit him. Not many people had seen a real live miracle before. They wanted to see him for themselves and ask him so many questions, but he was just beginning to understand what had happened to him. We were thrilled. He was trying to adjust to things we had been living with for almost a month. He needed time. He told me he was determined to be well enough to go to church on Easter Sunday.

"Easter Sunday was over three weeks ago, Honey," I tried to tell him gently. He was shocked.

Bruce had a lot of adjustments to make over the next days, not the least of which was regaining his strength. First, it was a big deal for him to be able to hold his own water cup. Then he sat up with assistance, then stood with a walker, and with physiotherapists hovering, eventually shuffled down the hallway, constantly amazing staff with how quickly he was recovering!

Chapter Nineteen

Day 29

We gathered the pictures and get-well cards posted on the cork bulletin board in Bruce's room and said good-bye to the great staff in the ICU, and Bruce was moved to a regular ward. It was bittersweet, I must say. Leaving that part of the hospital meant he was no longer in critical condition, which was amazing! However, after spending every single day (and a lot of nights) there for nearly 30 days, it was becoming a second home to me. The nurses were like old friends, and I was going to miss them—not to mention Bruce's spacious private room!

Some Christians feel like we can't be thankful for medicine or doctors because somehow that would downplay the miracles God performs. Others are the opposite and want to give all the credit to modern science.

I honestly cannot say enough about the staff and administration at the Lethbridge Regional Hospital! They were heroic, dedicated, intelligent, professional, caring, and passionate about saving my husband's life. The management was unbelievably accommodating to our circumstance and to the great many people who loved Bruce and just wanted to be near him. Bishop Todd had spent many hours in there and in other ICUs over the years praying for sick folks and said that he had never been treated so well as he was during this season. They extended grace and understanding to us in our time of need, and we are so grateful. They played such an unbelievable role in the healing of my husband and did everything medicine and science could do to save his life, and yet they still made room for us and our belief in God to help do what science couldn't. The doctors were of the highest calibre, and I feel honoured to have witnessed them work with such diligence and wisdom for my husband.

I know God healed my husband, His hand was ridiculously evident, but I also know that the ICU team were a huge part of that too, and I want to be sure to honour their expertise, diligence, and tireless work! We heard for weeks afterwards from a variety of sources that nearly all of the doctors involved in Bruce's care were calling his survival a miracle. A couple of medical staff independently suggested that Bruce was quite possibly the sickest person to have ever survived in the history of the Lethbridge hospital. Another doctor who we knew personally visited Bruce throughout the experience and, being sure that no one could live through what he was experiencing, said later that in his entire practice he had never, ever, seen a person that sick recover!

It was sad to say goodbye to them, but it was time to move on to the next stage for us, the surgical ward where Bruce would wait for procedures to close his wounds and repair his leg with skin grafts.

The road to recovery was not over, but I think the story is better told now by my husband himself.

Part Two
Bruce

Chapter Twenty

"**D**id you have a near-death experience? Did you have any visions or encounters with Jesus? Did you go to heaven?"

I can still see the anticipation in people's eyes when they ask me these questions, and I totally understand why. I was effectively in a coma a hair's breadth from death for three long weeks, with tens of thousands of people praying for me 24/7, and with miracles occurring throughout my body over that time. It's not unexpected that some would assume there's a good chance I saw Jesus or some angels or something supernatural! I actually feel a little bit apologetic to them, because even as I write this, I simply don't recall ever having had any such experience. I like to joke that the Church is to blame! You see, they prayed so hard that I never actually died!

I've asked the doctors this question a number of times: "Was there a point where I actually died?"

"No, Bruce. Your heart, although it nearly flat-lined a good number of times, never actually ever stopped," the doctors said.

I guess that's a good thing, right?

In fairness, it's probably best that I didn't actually leave my body and have some incredible encounter with Jesus or heaven. If I'd had, maybe I wouldn't have wanted to come back to earth. I imagine heaven is so glorious and amazing (and I don't mean just the incredible beauty but the joy unspeakable, the absence of tears and death, being face to face with Jesus, and experiencing the incredible love of God, forever and ever and ever and ever...) that seriously, who would ever want to come back from that? But as the Apostle Paul said in his opening remarks to the church in Philippi, "I am torn between the two: I desire to depart and be with Christ, which is better by far; but it is more necessary for you that I remain in the body" (1:23,24). And so for the sake of my family and especially my little children, it is better by far to be here with them than to have them grow up without their daddy. I truly feel so blessed to still be able to have the opportunity to raise them, and I hope to show them a good example of a father and a husband, God being my helper.

Waking Up

Now a question I *can* answer is what do I remember from those days when I began to wake up. Oh, those were crazy, trippy days! My first memories are of dreams—dreams where I typically became stuck in some place and couldn't move. It was actually pretty frustrating!

I later came to realize that some of those "dreams," or parts of them, were some strange combination of real events happening in the ICU room, with different backgrounds and scenery—kind of like when they use a "green screen" in movies, if you know what I mean. The dreams always seemed to happen in the evening or at night—well, at least in my frame of reference it was night. (Who knows what time it was?) I knew I was in a hospital of sorts, and in the evenings, I would get into a wheelchair and wheel over to the games/arcade room where all of us patients (mostly younger people and even some kids) all joined in a virtual reality simulation where we would play together or against each other. Inside that place, I would walk around a bit and then, sure enough, somehow get stuck in something. Every time.

I think one time I was trapped in a workout facility of sorts, and I couldn't seem to motion to people to help me out of my stuck position. Another time, once again stuck in some place, it began to snow and get cold. Nobody seemed to notice or care. Eventually someone came by—

someone I thought people should actually be afraid of—and he or she would help me get out and bring me a jacket to keep me warm. (I'm pretty sure in real life it was a nurse attending me—I can remember seeing the same face later, once I was fully coherent.)

Another time, I remember getting in trouble from the director of the institution that I was somehow in, for escaping out of my room, getting into my wheelchair, zooming down the long polished floors of the corridor, and hiding behind a cart stacked high with hospital linens. It was all so real! Yeah, those really were tripped-out times for me indeed!

And so the "dreams" went on, but with increasing levels of reality each time. Sometimes they involved being in different cities, which interestingly enough moved closer and closer geographically to my home city of Lethbridge, Alberta. They began with me being transported in an injured state in the back of a truck in Mexico (a leg wound as I recall), to being on a fishing boat in stormy waves off the coast of Hawaii while nursing a sting in my leg from some kind of fish. Then they moved to slow-motion sky-diving over the West Coast of British Columbia with a bunch of friends, where once again I had an injury in my leg and was so weak that the others played a game without me while I just guarded home base.

On and on it went, including one funnier dream where I was part of a practical joke in the city of Prince George, B.C. with my pastor, Bishop Todd Atkinson. I was to pop out of a coffin during a certain moment in the marriage ceremony that he was going to perform. It was the groom's idea, and yeah, we all thought it was going to be really funny. Maybe you had to be there.

The locations shifted through other parts of B.C. from the city where I grew up near beautiful Okanagan Lake with its green hillsides of orchards and vineyards, and finally across the jagged snow-topped Rocky Mountains all the way back to the windy prairie city of Lethbridge. I think back on those memories and they're so funny to me, because as the days went on (I'm unsure how much time it actually took to fully awaken), when I gradually began to think more clearly and when I heard people's voices around my bed in the ICU room, I knew them. I could see them with me and around me, and I knew I was in a hospital bed, but as I mentioned before, the background was different.

While He Lay Dying

We were in a classroom surrounded by desks or in a forest of snow-covered pine trees or in a living room I almost recognized. It was wild! Sometimes my room was my parent's family room back in Kelowna, where friends were having a party to celebrate my survival, and I wondered why a janitor person kept moving around the room cleaning. That seemed a bit unusual for my parents, who usually did that kind of thing themselves.

For a while, I even thought I was a kid, and just to the right of my room I saw a big white freezer where they stored the frozen ice treats for all of the patients in the ward...just out of reach. And yeah, well, in case you're wondering, there were no frozen ice treats. I hallucinated those. In reality, I actually must've been longing for something to put in my mouth because the tracheotomy puncturing my throat didn't permit me to ingest any food or water by mouth, not even for the first week after waking up, lest it accidentally go down the wrong pipe so to speak, and into my lungs—but more on that later.

Now the last conscious thing I remember before waking up in the ICU was being in the ultrasound room in the Lethbridge hospital. I had just finished having the scan done, and the technician mentioned he saw some fluid in my leg. Then the ambulance attendants left, their work being done.

It's fascinating how some types of drugs work. It was approximately one in the afternoon on Saturday when I had the ultrasound and seven in the evening when I had my first surgery, but the sedatives they gave me seemed to wipe out my memory retroactively to 1:00 pm, so those six hours in between are entirely gone.

Anyway, after the ultrasound, well, I woke up...three weeks later, that is.

Chapter
Twenty-one

—ᚷᚾ—

I Find Out the Truth

"**F**lesh Eating Disease?! Are you serious?!?! You mean it wasn't a pulled hamstring? You're telling me I've been asleep for the past three weeks?!?!?! … What city am I in?"

Yeah, those were some of my reactionary thoughts when I eventually found out the truth about what had happened during the three weeks that I was in an induced sleep. *That's crazy,* I thought. I went in with what I thought was a pulled hamstring, and apparently, it was a whole lot more than that! At least I didn't have to feel badly anymore about being sick during the birthday party preparations. (In fact, I suspect that I'll never, ever be accused of having a "man cold" again.)

It was all so surreal. I desperately tried to sort out which part of the hallucinations, or "dreams" I'd been having, were actually real. They say it's very normal when coming out of such a prolonged induced sleep, and what with the vast amount of medications given during that time, which my body was still trying to expel via round the clock dialysis, it was no wonder I was confused. On top of that, due to the memory-erasing side effects of the induced-sleep medicine, Lara, and those allowed in my room in those days, had to repeat the truth about my situation to me for three days until I could actually remember it! They had some fun with that.

While He Lay Dying

Everyone seemed so excited to see me—like, really excited. *I must've been pretty sick*, I thought. I didn't realize that I still wasn't quite out of the woods yet—I was now conscious but still on a lot of medication including heavy antibiotics to eradicate any residual infection. Lara gently laid her hand on my arm and moved her face closer so I didn't have to turn my neck, which still had tubes inserted. "Do you want to know what happened to you?"

Seeing me nod my head (I couldn't speak because of the tracheotomy) she said, "Honey, you had flesh eating disease. You've been very, very sick, but you are getting better. You have been unconscious for three weeks!"

Apparently, I'd go all bug-eyed, incredulous at what I was being told.

My friend Jep asked, "Do you want to see your feet?" and I'd make an expression on my face that kind of said, "My feet?? What do my feet have to do with this? It was only in my leg, wasn't it?" Come to think of it, I hadn't actually seen my feet and I was quite curious as to why they'd ask me that, so I indicated I wanted to see them. When I saw my absolutely disgusting feet, all black and purple and scabby, I'd once again go bug-eyed and quickly indicate for them to cover them up please. It was abundantly clear that any foot-modelling career was temporarily on hold, to say the least.

Lara said they had to repeat this revelation several times, the whole scenario playing out the next day all over again! Me not knowing what happened, them telling me the truth, and me going all bug-eyed and seeing my feet and going bug-eyed again—but by the third day, when they had to repeat it once more, it was becoming kind of humorous to them.

"Wait for it…here it comes…here it comes…ah, the bug eyes! Hey, let's ask him if he wants to see his feet, haha! Yeah, wait 'til he sees those, then he'll really go bug-eyed!"

Ah, I'm just glad they could laugh about it! I don't mind them having some good laughs at my expense—not after what they had to go through! I mean, they had to endure a rollercoaster of events and emotional trauma, and I just got to sleep through it all. So although my recovery seemed long, with some difficult aspects, I think I still got the easier part of it.

And oh, sometimes people ask me how I felt when I woke up. I've seen pictures of how weak my body was, and I'm reminded of how much rest I needed. Each time I see them I'm like—oh yeah, that's true, I was really weak, wasn't I. So I do remember it, but it wasn't actually my predominant recollection of that time. Rather, I just remember how amazingly good I felt in my soul. So refreshed, so deeply full—it's hard to explain. I honestly felt amazing! Perhaps, I wonder, if it simply has to do with the thousands upon thousands of people all around the world, all praying for me. Prayer really does work—because of the One we pray to!

Overwhelmed

Thousands, even tens of thousands of people were praying for me? I thought.

It was all so overwhelming. Lara talked to me even though I couldn't talk back. "Bruce, this is amazing! We keep hearing from more every day," Lara said. "I don't know how they even heard about the illness, but people keep sending messages to say that they are praying for you. They even wake up in the middle of the night thinking about you and with a desire to pray for you."

Wow. Who were they?

"There's a real mix of people. A lot of them say they had never really prayed for anybody like this before. Some of them haven't been to church in years, and some of them are leaders of organizations who can send out emails to hundreds or even thousands of people who will pray the same day."

That's incredible, I thought. *For me? Why would so many pray for me?*

"It's crazy the number of people who said they started to pray for you and then suddenly remembered times in their past when they felt like God didn't answer their prayers, or when they were all alone in a hospital room with a sick child or a dying brother and nobody came and prayed with them," she said, rubbing lotion on my arms. The combination of swelling up one hundred pounds and then shrinking back down and at one point being covered with blisters from a drug reaction had really affected my skin. It felt like I was painlessly shedding an entire layer all at once. Her touch was soothing.

While He Lay Dying

"A few people have said that it was like the Lord woke them up to pray for you but then instead took them through painful memories of disappointment. But as they talked to Him and cried about the hurt they felt, He somehow touched their hearts and lifted off the pain they had carried for so many years. Then they prayed for you again."

She moved to the opposite side of the bed to reach my other arm and gently rubbed it with a dry facecloth before reaching for the lotion again.

"There are prayer groups in places where we don't even know anyone. Honestly! Who are these guys? I don't know." She was getting excited now. "Eight Inuit villages, some Mexican villages, Mongolia, a group in Croatia...and your name was brought up in churches on Sunday morning all over the place—Vegreville and Red Deer and Moose Jaw and Saskatoon and Montreal and Cranbrook and Armstrong and Toronto and Kansas City and Pretoria and Las Vegas and Redding and Phoenix and cities in Africa and India and South America...I can't even pronounce the names of all these places. I think Antarctica is the only continent we haven't heard from."

As Lara's account describes, my story somehow caught fire and spread to so many people, all across our city and across Canada and even throughout the world. The Spirit of God seemed to impress so many people to pray that I would live and not die. It was quite overwhelming to wake up to, as you can probably imagine.

Everybody seemed excited to see me. And I do mean everybody—not just Lara and my brother and my parents and in-laws and my friends and my church, but even the nurses and the doctors. Staff members said my survival was so astounding, so miraculous, and the support for me was so far beyond anything they'd ever seen for an individual in the hospital, that they had to go see for themselves. Lara heard nurses saying they hoped their shift assignment allowed them to either meet this person they'd heard about or actually get to take care of him while he was conscious and to see what he was like.

I vividly remember my friends coming to see me. Some tentatively peeked around the door; others barged right in. With tears in their eyes or a look of jubilation or relief or excitement—or all of those at once, they stood by my bed and stared at me—conscious, alert, and interacting with them. Their expressions conveyed that they were staring into the face of a living miracle. It was wonderful for me to behold, because alongside amazement and relief was something else—something far greater—love. Each word or touch conveyed so much caring. It was a very special time, one that I recall with fondness and much emotion. I felt then that I'd grown so deeply, so profoundly in their hearts, the likes of which is difficult to develop in even the best of days and through much effort. As I lay there, weak but full, I'd be so joyful each time anyone would visit. I felt so happy and honoured to know them, and they were just glad I was alive!

Chapter Twenty-two

_⎯⋀⋀⎯_

My Family

My parents, who live nine hours away in Kelowna, B.C., were already in Lethbridge when I went into the hospital. They had come for a brief visit to celebrate two birthdays—Keziah's 4th and my mom's 70th—as well as Vivia's baby dedication ceremony. My brother Mark and my cousin David, who is very close, immediately flew in upon hearing the news that I was in critical condition; however, both of them had taken all the time off work they could, so they'd had to tear themselves away to go back to their jobs while I was in my most critical state. My parents, who own a small business, had also briefly returned to Kelowna to take care of some essential business items so they could stay longer when they came back.

Mom told me later, "Words cannot possibly describe the pain of leaving you behind. After a short visit at the hospital (unbeknownst to you), and promising to return in a week or so, we said our good-byes and we tore ourselves away to embark on our long drive home. I felt my heart being torn apart inch by inch! But even amidst all the turmoil, there was an inner awareness of the Lord being in control."

When the doctors decided to wake me up to see how my body would respond and my family received a phone call that I was starting to regain consciousness, my brother and my mom, having finished what she had to do, jumped into his car and raced back to see me! (My brother had a 48 hour break between shifts, close to 20 of which was spent driving.) The truth is, my mom doesn't like to travel without my dad, especially in poor weather, but since he simply had to stay behind (he came a few days later), she decided she could not wait and left right then, in spite of weather reports that predicted a snowstorm in Alberta.

In this part of the world, snowstorms often blow down from the mountains and completely white-out roads, temporarily removing all visibility as well as any hope of spring; hence most people think twice about such a trip if there's a forecast of snow. It didn't seem to stop her this time, however, nor my brother, who was determined to make the nine-hour drive in about six!

When a car with blue and red flashing lights pulled Mark over—I guess that's bound to happen when you're going as fast as he was—he explained to the officer that his brother was in the ICU.

"He has flesh-eating disease!" my mother added, leaning over from the passenger seat. (I've since found that the phrase "flesh-eating disease" seems to command a fair bit of attention. It can even come in quite handy at times.) When the officer heard the reason, he was very kind and let him go with just a warning.

My mom's last memory of me was of her swollen son lying comatose in a bed, surrounded by nurses and technicians, being totally dependent on a machine to breathe for him and with tubes inserted everywhere, going in all directions. Oh, the grief a parent must go through when watching a child die. I wish it would never happen to anyone. But you can imagine the joy and tears when she finally got to see me awake and I could interact with her—how I remember that moment! My mom and I have always been especially close. We have fairly similar personalities, so we understand each other and I was so glad for her that we were now on the other side of this ordeal.

And then, when my dad walked in a few days later, I realized again how much I love him. With a quiet strength, gracious wisdom, and a solid faith, he's a man who opens his mouth to speak less often than most, but when he does, you would do well to listen. While growing up, he tried to instill these qualities into my brother and me by telling us his favourite stories of great faith and courage and of times when God miraculously intervened in people's lives. And here, many years later, my dad now has yet another such story to tell. They tell me that during the crisis, he was how I've always known him to be—a rock. People to this day still talk about his quiet strength and deep faith that God would answer everyone's prayers, even when things seemed the darkest in those grim days. He is truly and without question a great man and someone I am deeply grateful for in my life.

As for seeing my brother—that was a very special moment indeed. You see, my brother and I have never really been that close. We're complete opposites—almost as opposite as brothers can get. For example, I'm a guy who tends to be quite logical and left-brained; hence, I like math and science. I'm athletic and play all kinds of sports. My brother on the other hand, is extremely musical and artistically gifted in every way you can think of and isn't very interested in playing sports or games. Suffice it to say, we had difficulty understanding or even appreciating each other's differences growing up, although we both enjoyed watching action flicks and Kung-Fu movies together, but who doesn't, right?

It also didn't help that I was a real pest to my brother when we were younger. He was so kind and trusting and innocent that he was easy to bug, and as the younger brother, bug I did. And I was smart enough to be able to hide my behaviour from my parents. I definitely regret the way I treated him as it eventually formed a rift between us. It took years for me to regain his trust, but back then as a kid, I just didn't know any better, nor did I realize how much it would cost me later.

We had managed to patch things up in recent years to a reasonable level, but we still weren't as close as either of us wanted to be. However, this is where almost-near-death experiences can come in handy! I say that in a lighthearted manner, but it's very true. When death comes to the forefront of a person's mind, whether through having to face it themselves or simply watching someone else close to them go through it, things come into perspective very quickly. Far less important at that point are some of the offenses and disappointments from the past, not to mention the multitude of other comparatively minor issues we encounter in life. Somehow, facing the possibility of death seems to make us conscious of the things we value, as well as the things we *should* value.

While I was unconscious, my brother joined Todd in the all-night vigils in my room. He had a lot of time to think about our relationship, and he conveyed to Todd that reconciliation with me was something that he earnestly desired. He was committed to it. When I woke up, I noticed a change in his heart. For the first time in many years, he seemed happier, more alive—and toward me, softer. The barriers were down. He was gentle and tender hearted, like I remember him being as a child. I hadn't seen him that way in a long time. It was wonderful! I remember how he'd take care of me in the hospital. As the congestion in my lungs was clearing, I coughed up bloody mucous that came out of the trach. Apparently, it was not a pretty sight, but hiding any sense of discomfort, Mark wiped it away with a warm wet cloth and cleaned me up.

Sometimes, while I lay there fatigued from the effort of trying to breathe or raise my arm or talk, he stroked his fingers through my hair. That may sound strange, and it isn't how typical friends or brothers behave, I suppose, but at the time, it was the best feeling in the world. I'd just lay there and enjoy it, appreciative for our friendship that had somehow turned a corner. It's too bad it took me almost dying to get us there—but I'll take it.

As I'd lay there in my ICU bed alone, I would find my thoughts occasionally glancing in the direction of what my family had to go through and suffer. The emotions were too much to bear, and I would quickly jump back from them like a hand getting an electric shock. Even to this day, imagining what my close-knit family, including my extended family and friends, had to endure seeing me during the worst parts of the illness and hearing the reports, which offered so little hope—it's still very painful to think about. A parent watching their child die, a mother wondering whether she'll have to raise her children alone, a wife facing the real possibility of losing her best friend and soul mate. Awful! For quite a while afterward, I even deliberately avoided looking at any pictures of myself from that time, simply because I couldn't bear to think of what those who loved me had to go through during those three long, surely horrendous weeks. In fact, it wasn't until five months later that I finally agreed to see people's pictures and videos. They were not fun to look at. I still think I got the easier end of the deal. They had to go through three hellish weeks, while I got to have a nice long nap.

Lara

Speaking of people who had to go through the worst of it, let me tell you about my wife, Lara. Oh, let me tell you about Lara—she is utterly amazing! Of course, at this point in the book, I'm sure that's not exactly coming as a revelation to you. But yeah, Lara is my soul mate, my best friend, and my favourite person in the whole world.

I won't take a bunch of time to tell you about my perspective of how we met, but let me just say this: I had waited and wondered for a long, long time for the answer to a certain question. It was not "Who could I spend the rest of my life with?" but "Who could I not spend the rest of my life without?" And Lara was that girl, through and through. From the very first night we spent time together in that Boston Pizza restaurant—I can still vividly remember the booth we sat in while we talked and how the rest of the world disappeared—I was riveted with her. Not only was she very beautiful on the outside, she was just as beautiful on the inside. She is truly a gem; I am a man who gets to say proudly without hesitation that "I married up!" I guess I'm tickled when Lara says the same thing about me—that she married up! But I suppose it's a good thing when both people feel they married up, isn't it?

So, it was absolutely relieving and reassuring every time I saw Lara walk into my hospital room. I needed her so much those days. Emotionally, she was such a strong support for me. Sometimes when she came in a little later than usual because of errands she had to run or the children's needs that couldn't wait, those extra minutes seemed like hours and hours. I just couldn't wait until the moment I'd see the first glimpse of her walking through the door. *Ahhh, Lara's here...everything is okay now.* I was glad that on most days, she was able to visit me a number of times a day, and I soon grew to know the exact sound of her footsteps coming toward my door. That was a good sound, indeed.

Chapter
Twenty-three

∿

Many Lives Touched and the Themes in My Heart

Now it seems that my ordeal had an unpredictable level and scope of impact all over, in so many people's lives. When my family and friends visited me, I heard how my ordeal had affected not just their lives, but so many lives, all over the globe (oh, it was so great to see so many of my close friends too, of course!! Wow, I can't express it adequately. Lots of tears and lots of laughs! I have the best friends in the world, hands down.). Although the things they were telling me were astonishing and almost incomprehensible, what was especially fascinating was that they all seemed to involve themes that were particularly dear to my heart!

For example, one of the themes I love is *reconciliation*—that is, relationships and the restoration of people's love toward each other. I heard so many stories of this happening as people would pray for me. God stopped them in their prayers and convicted them that they needed to get right with certain people in order for their prayers to be effective. And they would respond to God's gentle prod and He would do amazing things in people's relationships.

Another theme is *revival*—the idea of people's faith coming alive again to God. And I heard many, many stories of people's faith awakening and their hearts being stirred to pray like they hadn't before or hadn't for a long time. This event led some people's children to return to God, for others' faith in God to increase and for many Christians all over to realize the incredible power of prayer. So many people were encouraged when they noticed that God responded to them.

On that note, another theme I deeply love is *prayer*. While I was a pastor at our church, before my wife and I were led back into the field of education, one of my areas of oversight was prayer. I had actually tried to set up a prayer schedule, where around the clock, 24/7, people would pray for revival in our church and in our city. It went okay, but it never quite got the interest we were hoping for. But there, as my body lay dying, the church signed up for 24/7 prayer! I have the actual list that was put in the ICU waiting room, where people signed up for time slots to pray for me. There wasn't a single period of time in those three weeks that did not have people's names written in, committing to pray for me. It's so amazing how God does things! He fulfills the desires of our heart—desires that He gave us in the first place—in unimaginable ways!

Children! Investing in children and seeing them reach their full potential is also a huge passion I have! (I've been a teacher for over 15 years.) It was remarkable to hear the number of stories from parents whose children constantly reminded them to pray for me—children who didn't even know me—and of how they would weep as they did. Amazing! (When I had a chance to share in our Sunday school program afterwards, I asked how many kids had known of my situation and prayed for me throughout that time. Nearly every single hand of the 70 or so kids went up!) There's honestly so much I could say on this point, but at the very least let me say that it seems to me that God endeared my situation in children's hearts to encourage them with a soon-coming miracle. He also wanted to simply remind me that He is the one who formed me and made me who I am, including giving me a God-given passion and concern for children and desire to see them become all that He created them to be.

There are other themes as well, such as *unity* and *thanksgiving* and *surrender to the lordship of Christ* that were highlighted in people's lives, but there was one theme that was highlighted to me most strongly throughout this time. All my life I'd been a striver, trying to fulfill those legitimate God-dreams of mine (revival, prayer, etc.) and yet always coming up short. It was as if the Lord sent me a private message, saying, "You can't do it in your own strength! You tried, but your efforts didn't go very far. But here, watch this! If you let Me, I can do it through you."

He placed those passions there in me—and He brought them to fruition. Although physically I was weak and not able to get enough food in me to keep up with my body's regeneration, I felt full inside. I understood what it meant to be fed with something greater than food (and I do enjoy food!) I think of the story of when Jesus sent His disciples into town to get some food but stayed behind to minister to a woman whose soul was impoverished. When they came back and offered him food, He said, "I have food to eat that you know nothing about." When His disciples said to each other, "Could someone have brought him food?" He simply replied, "My food...is to do the will of him who sent me and to finish his work" (John 4:34). I think that's kind of how I felt—my soul was so satisfied, so nourished from the stories of the good things God had done in so many people's lives. How could I not be utterly thankful? My heart was full.

Where Did That Muscle Go?

Now as I mentioned, my soul felt amazing—so amazing in fact, that I actually have to try and remember how weak my body was when I came to. Of course, when I see a picture now of what I looked like then, instantly I'm like, oh yeah... right.

My body had gone through the ringer. For you to understand the depths to which it fell, I'll briefly describe the *place* from which it fell. Before contracting flesh-eating disease (FED as my friends came to call it as they'd pray for me), I was actually in good shape. Every week I'd usually lift weights a few times, and try to go for a run or a swim. After having played lots of sports all my life, I was pretty strong. As a point of reference, before going into the ER I remember being able to bench press 225 pounds for a full set and do a single arm curl of about 45 pounds, so I had a pretty good muscle base—although with about 25 pounds of extra fat on me too, haha. (Though that came in handy, as it turns out.)

While He Lay Dying

When I woke up, I found that I couldn't even lift my left arm above my head. That was disconcerting. I tried to move the sheet off my chest because I felt hot, but I didn't have the strength. In fact, merely trying to point to it in an effort to ask for help took all the strength I could muster. Crazy! Every little move in bed, even trying to shift about or, later on, to bring a glass of water to my mouth, was work. My body weakened quickly because of the muscle atrophy due to inactivity and the tremendous amount of energy it required to try and fight off the infection, as well as to heal the three sites on my leg where they'd done large surgeries. I received food intravenously and by a naso-gastric tube 24/7, but it simply couldn't keep up to my body's demands. There's just no way a guy my size could ingest enough nutrition and calories to keep up with what my body needed. The doctor even said that it was good that I had such a good muscle base before—and the extra fat! See Lara? It *is* good that I eat fast food sometimes…and some donuts and chocolate on occasion, *cough, cough.* (I suspect that sentence won't make it through the editing phases of this book…Maybe I'll just reinsert it after each edit! And if you're reading this, then success!)

Almost everyone would think that having three full weeks of sleep, instead of working or having any responsibilities, would be just awesome! However, when it also involves having multiple major surgeries and a bout with FED and sepsis, not to mention all of the other associated complications, waking up was actually rather difficult!

The first task was trying to figure out a way to communicate with everyone. I couldn't talk because the trach tube inserted in my throat was rendering it impossible to use my vocal chords. All I could do initially was nod or motion with my hands to try to get my point across. Then someone suggested that I try using a paper and pen. *Of course! Why hadn't we thought of that?!* So, Lara fetched a pad of paper and a pen for me, and I tried to write.

Hahaha…oh boy, this was sooo not going to work! The first problem was actually trying to grip the pen properly! For some reason, my fine motor skills just weren't there, and so it took me forever (it seemed like it anyway) to hold it properly. I dropped it or couldn't point it in the right direction. I saw the expressions of the people I was with and I could tell they had to restrain themselves from helping me.

Inside they must have been hoping I would ask for help, but I was stubbornly determined to do this on my own—I mean surely I can pick up a pen, right?! Eventually I'd get it in position in my fingers. But then, the second obstacle interfered—my uncoordinated eyes!

My eyes were still getting back to normal and weren't quite working together properly (that's an understatement), so when I attempted to put the pen on the paper and write, it would land just off the actual paper. Strange. So, I'd try it again, and sure enough—not even on the page. Then I tried closing each eye separately to see what was going on, and surprise, surprise—each eye was seeing things from a significantly different perspective. *Oh, that's just fantastic.* And so, I finally decided to pick one eye to go with and close the other. Ah, this time my pen hit the page!

Enter obstacle number three. When I wrote the first word, all my letters piled up on top of each other. It was like using a typewriter with a cartridge that didn't advance so the letters all stamped in the same place. All I seemed to produce was a whole lot of ink on one spot on the paper. *Yeah,* I thought—*this is pretty much useless.*

But Lara figured out what to do—she slowly moved the paper while I was writing! Haha…sounds too funny, but it's true! I have no recollection of her moving it, so stealthy was she, but that's when obstacle number four appeared—none of my letters were actually *legible*. Likely for some medical reason unknown to me (I'll bet they have a term for it, mind you. I feel like I got a diploma in medical terminology through this.) my fine motor skills weren't working properly yet, so I couldn't even draw an "a" or "b" or any other letter. I remember hoping it wasn't permanent or something. Okay, scratch the paper and pen idea. *Maybe we'll revisit that one later,* I thought, *because presently it's not really helping. In fact, it's probably just making everyone else—and me—more frustrated.* That's when I had what I thought was a brilliant idea…*a tablet!* Of course, why hadn't I thought of that earlier?!

So, Lara brought my iPad the next day, but apparently, fine motor skills are needed for tablets too. *No go.* On the first attempt my father-in-law held the iPad within reach of my propped-up hand and toward the side with the eye I wasn't closing. I hit a letter that I had no intention of hitting, and the people with me started guessing at the word like we were playing a game of charades.

While He Lay Dying

"O. Open? Do you want us to open the curtains?"

"Off? I think he wants something off. Maybe he wants the fan turned off. Do you want the fan off, Bruce? Are you cold?"

I shook my head and made another attempt to hit the "I."

"J. OJ? You want some orange juice. Funny guy. You can't drink anything…OJKLI?"

"What?"

I'd try to hit backspace and just ended up hitting the letter "P."
PPPPPPPPPPPPPPPPPPPPPPPPPPPPPPPPPPPPPPPPPPPPPPPPPPPPPP

As you can tell, that wasn't very helpful in my attempts to successfully communicate. As hard as I tried, I couldn't make my finger go where I wanted it to. For someone who won speed-typing contests back in school, this was disturbing. As patient as everyone was, it was readily apparent the iPad wasn't going to work. Shelve the tablet idea as well.

At this point, by default obviously, I switched back to focusing more on using my voice again. A couple days had gone by and they had decided I was ready for a bit of an upgraded trach. At first they told me that I wouldn't be able to talk, but if they did a certain thing momentarily by covering up the opening on the front, my breath could be redirected through my vocal chords for a bit and I might be able to say a phrase. I listened to myself breathe on this new trach. *I actually sound a lot like Darth Vader.*

"We'll try it just this once for now, so take some time to think about what you want to say," the nurse cautioned.

"Make it good, honey!" Lara urged.

Being unable to speak gave me a greater sense of compassion for people who have to work very hard at making themselves understood. There were all sorts of thoughts locked inside me, but because I had been unconscious for so long, I admit I was unaware of how much those first words meant to Lara and family and friends. They had waited much longer than I had. They didn't know if I would be the same person, or if my brain would work the same way as it had before, or work at all. Had I taken more time to think seriously about the weight carried in those first words, I may have come up with something else, but as it turns out, they were exactly what everyone wanted to hear. I just thought about how much I sounded like Darth Vader and went for it.

"Axel...I am your faaaaather."

It was hard for her to hear me and Lara thought I said, "Luke...I am your faaaather," and perhaps I did. No matter. The words told people what they wanted to hear via my own unique sense of humour—I was back. Yes, it was the same old Bruce, his body attached by wires and tubes to machines, but the same guy was still in there. The power of five simple words! It gave me joy to see Lara smile.

Through Lara's Facebook postings the words travelled far and wide and people had a good laugh. One guy named Luke joked it had him worried for a minute, but he calculated our age difference and breathed a sigh of relief when he realized it did not compute (kidding). Besides endearing me to the nursing staff even more apparently, the story even worked its way into a children's day camp presentation and also resulted in someone from the church kindly purchasing a Darth Vader shirt for me, which I still wear with pride on occasion. That shirt is only second favourite to the shirt Lara and the kids got me on Father's Day, which read, "I survived Flesh-Eating Disease and all I got was this lousy t-shirt."

It turns out that although they said I would not be able to talk on that new trach—somehow I could! Apparently, my windpipe was large enough for me to still get a bit of air past the trach and through my vocal chords. So, if I timed it just right with my breaths, I'd be able to utter a sound or word at the beginning of the breath. If it sounds tricky or arduous, it was—but it worked! I'm kind of a determined guy, and hey, I didn't have much else to do. It took a while, but I was able to, word by word, speak a sentence and finally, finally, was able to communicate more significantly with all of my friends and family—and of course, the nurses, which can be very useful at times I assure you.

The Symbolism in My Body

It was in those early days, after waking up, that Bishop Todd began to tell me some of the things God had showed him and others during the weeks I was sleeping. To be honest, it was overwhelming. In a later chapter you'll be able to read his full take on my situation and what it meant for the Body of Christ at large—trust me, you don't want miss that—but needless to say, it left me knowing this story was not just about me. Not at all. My ordeal and miraculous recovery was a whole lot bigger than that and had a message of great promise for the Church far and wide.

Chapter
Twenty-four

–√\√–

Appreciation for the Medical Staff

A dressing change took three nurses in sterile garb at least 35 minutes. The three separate incisions—my entire calf and the side of my thigh, both about a foot long, and the full length of my hamstring, knee to bum—had not been sewn or stapled shut after surgery. (Squeamish alert) I remember staring with curiosity at my exposed pink calf muscle. It looked like one of those Body Works displays, where you'd look at a re-creation of a body minus its skin—just tendons, muscles, etc. For a science kind of guy, it was really quite fascinating, actually!

Fortunately, they weren't as painful as you might think, due to the huge doses of narcotic painkiller I was on. That medication helped me to endure the regular routine of the nurses lifting my leg up in a stirrup via a mechanized hoist so they could access my calf. They worked around all the machines and IV poles and lines going in (and out) of my body, turning me onto my side. It took a choreographed effort on the part of all three of them to do the changes on my wounds those days. The hard part for me was staying on my side when they were working on my thigh. I needed to lie still the whole time, but I barely had the strength to hold on to the rails, let alone maintain my balance. Thankfully, a nurse would help to hold me on my side each time so I could just manage. It's humbling to be dependent on others for practically everything, even to move my arm or change my position. Sometimes I felt like a helpless child, but they cared for me and spared my dignity (as much as possible.)

I actually appreciated the friendly banter between the nurses at times like this. Not only did it occupy my mind, but it was quite amusing. I found out that one of the guys had a reputation for eating all the goodies people brought in to thank the staff and that another nurse had appointed herself "guardian of the goodies," so that Doug wouldn't get them all, yet they still seemed to disappear anyhow. It had actually become a game.

For the record, Doug was a *great* nurse, as were all the others. In fact, I can't overstate how impressed we were by the dedication and expertise of all the many medical staff that helped me during my ordeal, from when I entered the ER that one Saturday until I was finally discharged. Though I firmly believe that God is the ultimate Healer and He alone is the source of all life and healing, including miracles, I also know that He works through people.

One of my passions is to see people come into their callings, and it amazes me how God puts skills and abilities and passions in every one of us. I appreciate that some are born with a curiosity about how the body works and how to fix it when something goes wrong. God has given them fine minds, able hands, and a desire to help people heal and regain function. I honour the dedication it takes to study and pursue medical excellence and the skills each technician, nurse, therapist physician, and researcher spent years of their life honing—not to mention the amazing ability to stay awake and alert, all night. I am so grateful for their contribution to my healing—especially the way they kept looking for one more thing they could possibly try, even when everything in their experience told them that I would not survive and they had run out of options. I particularly admire nurses and physician specialists who work in areas of healthcare where so many, if not most, of their patients succumb to their illnesses. It must take a great deal of courage to keep coming back to work and to allow themselves to care and fight for people who may not make it. How often my heart fills with thankfulness for their efforts and kindness.

More Miracles

We found out later that one experienced doctor who had treated many patients in critical condition had said that if I survived it would be the biggest miracle he had ever seen in his entire medical practice. Other doctors said similar things—and another doctor, we heard, had said it this way to a friend of ours: "[expletive]! That guy should be dead." Indeed, "miracle" and "miraculous" (and other words to that effect) were words used often by the medical staff.

Besides my actual survival, they also said that my recovery was "nothing short of stunning, without exaggeration." First, my wounds were healing amazingly well. I remember one nurse getting goose bumps when doing my daily dressing. "Can I take a photo of these?" she asked. "I train other nurses to do wound care, and these are healing so well!"

"Sure, have at 'er!" I said.

My creatinine levels kept dropping and dropping and dropping (lower is always good), so much so that they were now well below normal (100–120) and had reached 89! The doctor said that instead of having the kidneys of a 108-year old as expected at one point, I now had the kidneys of a 20-year old (half my age.) Incredible.

My lungs also recovered quickly. They had filled with blood, contracted pneumonia, and for a long time had been functioning 100 percent via machines, but soon the respiratory technicians were able to reduce the oxygen levels, all the while upgrading some of the trach apparatus as I could handle it. Within days, they pulled the trach out (that was unexpectedly painful by the way—ouch!!) and I was breathing on my own. This is how well my lungs recovered: after I was transferred to a regular ward, nurses performed the usual vital sign checks. Part of that was putting a plastic clamp of sorts on my finger. It measures *oxygenation*, the percent of oxygen in the air that your body is absorbing. The average person's levels are between 96 and 99 percent, but when they'd check me, my levels were typically at 100 percent. I remember one nurse remarking that nobody on the entire floor had numbers like that, not even the nurses. Amazing.

There was also concern from the medical team that the severe sepsis might have had a detrimental effect on my mental functions, especially when I woke up with those crazy eyes. Many medical staff believed my brain would probably suffer *permanent* damage through all of that and the effects would be noticeable. I remember a doctor specifically asking me if I'd noticed any mental diminishment, such as memory loss or gaps in thinking. I would ask Lara and my relatives and close friends if they noticed anything different there, because I didn't notice anything. They all said the same thing—you're the same Bruce we've always known. Just more handsome! (Okay, I made that last sentence up.) But as far as brain functions go, without exaggeration, I honestly feel noticeably clearer, sharper, and quicker in my thinking than when I first went in. It was like my entire insides, brain included, got a big lube job. Instead of being contaminated, they got a good overhaul and (arguably) even improved. In fact, by God's grace, only a few months after leaving the hospital I began writing a college level calculus curriculum for use in one of the world's largest online schools!

The whole recovery defied expectations. It was "stunning," in the medical staff's words, just as the previous miracles had been. It was at this point that one of the doctors relayed a comment from one of the specialists who had treated me, mentioning that he felt it was truly a miracle I had survived. The doctor agreed.

Walking Again…Sort Of

This one also went quickly in the medical profession's eyes, though still not quickly enough for me!

Patience is not one of my stronger virtues. I like to do things quickly, like, yesterday if possible! (Unless it's cleaning up the yard or taking out the garbage—then my wife kindly informs me that I tend to procrastinate…guilty as charged.) A week after waking up, and still in the ICU, I was feeling better and better each day and I felt raring to go! Although the truth is that I was still very weak and I just hadn't noticed. I could barely lift arms above my head!

"So I figure in one week I should be walking again and then in one week after that I can walk out of the hospital. Maybe I'll be ready to do the half-triathlon I did last year when it comes around in June again.

What do you think?" I asked the doctor, while trying to find the remote to adjust the incline of my bed.

A big smile appeared on his face, as he kind of just shook his head and said, "Dude…I'm just happy you're alive!"

A few days later, with the help of physiotherapists, I was able to take a few steps in the hall of the ICU. Apparently, I got an ovation as I emerged into the hall, but I don't remember because I was just so focused on holding on to the oversized walker. In the coming days I could walk more and more each day with the walker—I still remember the shaking of heads in amazement by some of the medical staff as I did a full lap of the ICU—my "victory lap," someone called it.

However, as good as my progress was, it turns out that the doctor was quite right about it taking longer than I projected. The ability to take little strolls in the hallway, gained with so much effort, was lost after skin grafts and surgery to close the wounds immobilized me again. It was a disappointing setback. Almost one full month after waking up, I was again unable to take the smallest of steps on my own. Learning to walk again was a frustrating process that involved my leg regaining strength and flexibility, with lots of rehab and physiotherapy, coping with considerable nerve pain in my feet, and more. Medical staff agreed I was apparently still progressing very, very rapidly—with much more rapid progress than they had seen in patients who were not nearly as sick as I had been. But it was not rapid enough for me.

Yet, through it all, since I experienced so much personally during that time, God did some amazing things in my heart. I'll talk about those in a little detail later, but on the book's website (located at the back of the book) you'll also see a video link where you can see me share more of this in person at my first full Sunday back at church. That was fun.

Chapter Twenty-five

—⎍⋏⎍—

Movin' On Up!

I t was a good day when they told me I was going to be transferred out of the ICU and into a regular ward. I mean, it was sad in the sense that I'd gotten to know many of the nurses and staff in the ICU and I likely wouldn't get to see them again, but on the other hand, it indicated that I was no longer so sick that they had to give me intensive care. It was definitely a graduation of sorts! And so, about a month into my ordeal, they brought the bed from the ward to mine in the ICU, and we transferred.

To be honest, I didn't transfer all that gracefully. You see, I was feeling better and better every day and beginning to regain my strength. On that particular day, perhaps bolstered by the thought that I was transferring out of the ICU, I felt especially confident in my improving strength. When a nurse and a hospital porter came to transfer me from the one bed to the next, I stopped them.

"I got this," I assured them. With great effort, I shuffled myself to the edge of my bed and then kind of flung my left arm and leg over, turning onto my front, so that now I was on the new bed, but on my hands and knees.

So far so good, right? Well, not exactly.

While He Lay Dying

Issue #1: I was now stuck and had no way to rotate myself to get to the required lying position. It took all my energy just to keep that position and to keep from falling.

Issue #2: I was wearing a hospital gown—you know, the kind that is solid in front, and entirely open at the back?—yeah, and entirely untied, I might add.

Issue #3: The nurse and attendant couldn't refrain themselves from laughing—loudly. I couldn't blame them.

So there I was, stuck on a bed, naked, bum up in the air, with two people laughing helplessly.

"It seemed like such a good idea at the time," I muttered. And then I joined them, howling in laughter. *What was I thinking with that?!*

I guess my strength still had a ways to go. *"Oh, how the mighty have fallen,"* I chuckled to myself.

Dinner Is Served

Oh—just before I talk about life in the main ward, let me mention one more thing. While I was still in the ICU, I remember my first days of getting to taste actual food again. It had been a full week after coming to my senses, and I was still not allowed any food or drink, not even water, because of the risks associated with the trach. I was desperate for some real food—anything at all—yet all I was allowed to "enjoy" at this point were these "water popsicles." A water popsicle is a tiny sponge on a stick that someone can dip into water and hand to a patient to suck on. Although I was grateful for the moisture in my mouth, it wasn't exactly like eating a steak sandwich. Anyway, things were looking up for ol' Brucey, 'cause I received great news that day.

"Go down to the grocery store and buy a case of Five Alive on your way home, okay?" I managed to whisper to Lara. "They are going to let me start drinking! Put some in the fridge so it will be cold." I could almost taste it! "Bring it with you in the morning—oh, and you can have some too!" Lara was so patient with me during my demanding phase back then…(the years since we got married, I mean).

"A whole case? You want me to buy a whole case?" She looked at me questioningly.

156

I nodded.

"If that's what you want, I will buy you a whole case of juice," she smiled. What a darling she truly is. Honestly.

In the morning, I took my first sip as she held it to my lips. It tasted...metallic! Yuck!! It turns out that certain kinds of medicine administered over prolonged periods of time can have a drastic effect on one's taste buds.

"Try putting some water in it," I croaked. Remember, I hadn't eaten anything in almost a month at that point.

I tasted it again. "A little more water..."

In the end, she diluted the juice with about 80 percent water, and it still tasted more like metal than the delicious fruit juice that I remembered, but at least I could drink it.

When I could breathe on my own and swallow well enough, I was allowed to have real food. At first, nothing tasted right because of the weird taste bud issue, but after a while, it began to improve and I looked forward to the sound of "the room service people" rolling their fine-smelling dinner trolleys down the hall. I don't usually mind the taste of hospital food anyway, but trust me, when you haven't eaten anything for over a month, even institutional food tastes like manna from heaven.

Chocolate on the Chart

Now a few days after I was transferred to the regular ward, the dietician came to visit me again. She handed me a piece of paper and asked if I could keep meticulous track of everything I ate for the next three days—breakfast, lunch, dinner, and all snacks.

"Sure!" I said, "Though may I ask why?" I was concerned that something was wrong.

Her reply confirmed it. "You're not eating enough."

I was surprised. I thought I was eating quite a bit now already. "Really?! How do you know?" I realized there must be something she was basing that on.

"Your weight is still dropping," she said, with noticeable compassion on her face. (Apparently, the bed I was on had a built-in weighing feature. *There's no privacy for the bed-ridden.*)

While He Lay Dying

I couldn't believe it. "I've been eating as much as I can!" I said, still finding it hard to believe. It was true—I was eating as much I could, trying to battle through the nausea from the various drugs I was on and keep from throwing up whatever I was eating.

"It's very important to get enough nutrition so that your body has the energy it needs to heal all those large wounds on your leg, not to mention just trying to sustain itself."

"But I *am* eating!" I protested.

"Unfortunately, it's not enough," she said gently.

It didn't help that my stomach had shrunk down to almost nothing after receiving only liquid food via tube for almost a month until I could swallow again. But I really had been trying. I went into the hospital at 237 pounds (I had weighed myself just days before), swelled up to 330 pounds, and at last weigh-in in the ICU, I was 205. I guess they had been taking my weight discreetly on the bed with the built-in digital scale, and it was apparently still dropping. (When we were tossing around potential titles for this book, I suggested, *How to Gain 100 Pounds In 4 Days...And Have People Love You for It.*)

I was curious what it was now and asked her if she knew. She said, "Let's just weigh you and see," and she hit a few buttons at the front of my bed. "...201 pounds."

"Wow," I managed. *Crazy,* I thought, as I shook my head. That was a weight I hadn't been at since my early 20s. (I often joke to people who want to lose weight that I know of a drastic weight-loss program that really works, but it's one I can't exactly recommend.)

So, for the next days I kept a detailed record of all foods taken in, and she came back with my calorie total—I think around 2,300 a day, which was still about 1,000 calories below what she felt I should be ingesting.

"Your nutrition isn't the issue," she said. "It's your calories. You need more calories."

"I could revisit my chocolate addiction," I joked. (I really, really like chocolate, for the record. Anyone who knows me will tell you that straightaway.) But to my surprise, she kind of shrugged her shoulders and raised her eyebrows; her facial expression and mild nodding telling me something like "Sure—that'd be okay, if it means it gets you more calories," and before I could say anything, she asked me if I liked chips!

"Are you serious?! I can eat junk food like chocolate and chips?!" I was both surprised and kind of excited! I knew where this was going. For the first time in my life, I was going to get a free pass to eat absolutely anything I wanted! And Lara would be powerless to say anything against it, haha. I could see it now—I'd be indulging myself with copious amounts of chocolate and, as Lara looked on disapprovingly, I'd whip out the phrase: "Doctor's orders, Sweetie."

The dietician said she was totally fine with me eating chocolate, and chips, so...I asked her if she would officially put chocolate on my chart, so my wife would believe me. And she did! On my official chart, it read "chocolate." *And thus began the single greatest season of my life...* Haha, okay not quite. But I could finally eat anything and everything I wanted. The only problem was I was so nauseated I didn't often *want* to eat! But unlimited chocolate...mmmm...*I will find a way.*

It turns out the dietician was right about the massive amount of energy my body used to heal itself. Not that I didn't believe her, of course, but I was surprised to find out how little weight I gained after ten straight days of eating absolutely everything I could muster. Even though applying all my willpower to ignore the nausea and packing in every morsel I could, after ten days I was still only up by *one pound*—but at least my weight wasn't going down anymore.

Indeed, my body desperately needed nutrition and rest to recover. I remember being so tired in those days. It wasn't helping that everyone wanted to come say hi and visit. I mean, I really felt so loved and honoured and thankful to have so many people come and visit me in the hospital—because some people spend their days in the hospital very lonely, it's sad—but on the other hand, the attention I was getting was exhausting. I felt like I wanted to show my gratitude to people for coming and to honour them for praying so hard, and loving my family during the crisis, but I needed time to rest. Finally the nurses stepped in and said that pretty much only immediate family and clergy were allowed to see me, hoping it would help me get my much-needed recuperation time.

Chapter Twenty-six

The Man in the Mirror

It was around that time when I looked in a mirror for the first time since waking up. The face looking back at me in the mirror looked vaguely familiar, but he was so very gaunt—and his beard! Wow, what a shock! Because my platelets had been so low and shaving carried the risk of cuts, they just let it grow. There was a problem though, because my breathing and feeding tubes needed to be taped in order to stabilize them. Tape doesn't stick well to beards, so somebody carefully cut little clearings in what otherwise was becoming a proper mountain man beard. And my hair! My hair, which hadn't been washed in over a month, fell from a central part and was pasted to my head like someone from the '60s. The kindness and love in my friends' and family's eyes had hidden my true appearance until then, and I was not prepared for who, or even what, I was looking at. Alas, it had to stay that way a while longer until I was healed up well enough to shave or take a shower, some 50 days after my last one.

While He Lay Dying

"Miracle Man"

A few days after I was transferred to the regular ward, they took me down to the operating room area to wait for my skin graft surgery. A nurse there came to check my charts, and when she saw my name she said, "Bruce Merz?...Oh, 'Miracle Man'!"

"Excuse me?" I asked.

"Miracle Man. That's what everybody in the hospital is calling you," she said as she flipped through the pages.

"You know about me?"

"Everyone knows about you," she said, smiling.

That surprised me! I hadn't heard that nickname before, but more importantly—I wondered how in the world this nurse had heard of me? As I'd mentioned earlier, my story spread throughout the hospital, and it seemed for a long time after my release, whether I went back to the hospital for a follow-up or when I had my appointment to check the skin grafts or even when I ran into a lab technician at my daughter's preschool graduation later, they would all know my story. *Incredible.*

I really think there were two major factors that caused my story to spread like wildfire in the hospital. The first of course, is the miraculous aspect of my situation. I experienced: 1) flesh eating disease; 2) severe sepsis; 3) six potentially fatal conditions all occurring at the same time (medically speaking there's no reason I should be alive, they said); 4) miraculous improvement in blood pressure, lung and kidney function; and 5) no loss of brain function, limbs, muscle or even toes. A "stunning" recovery.

The other big factor, just as important, was a demonstration of love. Love isn't so much talk as it is action, and the hospital staff working with my situation got to see love and support poured out on me as "they had never witnessed before in the history of the hospital." They saw a constant stream of hundreds of people visiting and praying for me 24/7 for weeks. They heard stories of how people had cared for my family in myriad ways and experienced the quality and character of our community firsthand. They felt the admiration and appreciation for all of their efforts. It's not surprising that it made such a lasting impact.

It was this supernatural dimension of God—true love—that when combined with the miracles, managed to reach the hospital staff's hearts and minds. And that's how the nickname "Miracle Man," as I was dubbed by the nurses and doctors who worked with me, came to be. It's a testament to the nature and power of the one true God who is alive and who is love itself and to His Church, the community and Body of Jesus Christ, which is His fullness and expression here on earth. Imperfect no doubt, yet the Church still shines forth with His radiant and irresistible love, mercy, forgiveness, and power poured out for all. Jesus is both the original and ultimate "Miracle Man."

Cheese Grating (Getting Skin Grafts)

So there I was, in the operating room, staring at the bright overhead light, my arms outstretched for an IV and blood pressure cuff. As the anesthetic dragged me into sleep, I thought about how much my wife and family and friends and I had been through and how much of the goodness of God we had seen since the last time I was in this room. I felt peace.

When I woke up, I felt pain! Lots of pain!! Wow, that hurt! It was the first time I recall feeling real, acute pain since I'd gone in. And not on my leg where the grafts were put. No, no! It hurt on my donor site, which was my right thigh. (They basically cheese-grate the donor site to get very thin slices of skin and then poke tiny holes in it so they can stretch them out and put them on the recipient site.)

"Um, more morphine, please!" Yeah, I took the maximum dose I was allowed that day!

So, for ten days I had a sort of cast on my left leg that prevented my leg from bending so that the grafts wouldn't move at all. It was ten long days of watching the second hand on the clock circle around and around, one tiny lurch at a time. Other than during my limited physiotherapy sessions, I spent the entire time lying still in bed. That's when I really began to miss my kids and longed to be home. Lara still visited twice a day as usual, and sometimes the kids came too. They spent a lot of time endearing themselves to the nurses in the station across from my room and being rewarded with cookies and juice boxes. I wanted to hold them and play with them, but when you're stuck in a hospital bed, unable to move around, it's not exactly the highest quality time spent with your kids, if you know what I mean.

Keziah took it well; she was old enough to understand what was going on and just enjoyed any time with Daddy she could get. She sat on the edge of my bed and asked a thousand questions, the way she always does.

My son Axel, however, took it harder. He had such a difficult time looking at me. I had lost almost 40 pounds and was still bedridden. My face was thinner, my hair was longer, my face had a bushy beard, and my vocal chords were still healing so I even spoke differently. Daddy just wasn't looking or acting or sounding like the daddy he knew, and it brought a level of discomfort to him and even resentment, I think.

It's not fair, Axel, I thought. *What happened to you wasn't fair, not fair at all. And now your daddy's been gone for so long—over a month already—and somehow your innocent and pure mind and soul has to interpret this as best as it can. Sin will try to get in there to get you to make wrong conclusions about this. God have mercy. God, pour out Your grace on him...*

Sometimes things happen in life that aren't our fault. I could think of nothing that I did to directly precipitate this crisis that affected their young lives so profoundly, but I knew God would provide grace. He always does. It's there for the taking. There were so many people who were specifically praying just for that aspect—our kids and that they'd be able to journey this remarkably well.

Note: Months later, after a specific and remarkable time of prayer for him, Axel's emotions received a full, instant healing. Literally in a moment, he returned to normal. The hardness and jadedness were gone, and only our sweet, gentle Axel remained. He was back 100%. Praise God! Praise God!!

The Skin Graft Test

After ten days, the plastic surgeon came to take the cast-thing (a "Zimmer splint," as I recall) off, but he left the removal of the bandages on my donor site to the nurses. I asked the surgeon, since he was a very nice doctor, if this would hurt.

"It's never hurt me once," he said.

I chuckled. "Thanks so much!" I said, using my sarcastic voice. "That is very reassuring."

"No problem, Bruce," he said, waving as he slipped out of the room.

Turns out it hurts like *crazy*. Not the cast part but the donor site.

"He always leaves when we get to this part," one nurse joked.

"That's because he wants to play good cop," the other one said.

I looked at her questioningly.

"We joke that we play good cop/bad cop, but it's not fair because he always gets to be the good cop." With her gloved hand she picked up tweezers and scissors from a sterilized package. "Sorry," she said and went to work, cutting and removing the bandages.

(If you're wondering why it hurts—and don't read this if you're overly squeamish—the bleeding from the donor site adheres to the special tissues they put around it, and at the right time, they peel them off to reveal the healing skin...Yeah, exactly—peel.) I grimaced and gripped whatever I could find while they did that. It seemed to take forever, as most painful things do. They said that I did really well—often there's just lots of screaming. Though I took a bit of comfort in the compliment, I was just glad that it was over!

Of course, the big question in my mind was how well were my grafts taking? I had two separate sites that required skin grafts: an eight-inch long by four-inch wide site by my left calf muscle, and nearly the entire back of my upper left leg, where the FED initially attacked. There was actually a third site on the left side of my upper left leg, about eight inches long, but it didn't require a graft because my leg had atrophied and shrunk so much by this point. They simply pulled the skin together there and stapled it closed. (My legs were so small that I could now wrap my thumbs and middle fingers around the biggest parts of my thigh, and they would overlap half way down the fingernails.)

I had mixed emotions in anticipation of what the plastic surgeon would say when he came back. He was basically coming to give the official assessment of how well the skin grafts were taking. (A skin graft is "taking" if the blood vessels beneath seem to have received the graft and are sufficiently nourishing the skin.) He returned a second time about six days later to assess the graft again and give his official "okay" or his official "gotta-redo." The first time he felt the graft was doing very well (so far so good, and consistent with how everything else in my body seemed to be doing), but then in the next few days when the nurses changed the dressings, they'd comment about some of the brown spots and this and that. I heard them wondering aloud if maybe they might have to redo parts of the graft, which apparently happens quite often with this procedure. We were told that a surprisingly high percentage of people have to have re-grafts, especially those whose bodies have been through the extreme stress of major infection, sepsis, and kidney and organ failure.

I told Lara about their comments and asked if she would post the request to Facebook so people could pray that we wouldn't have to redo those. I didn't want to have to go through that again if at all possible—not so much for the pain avoidance, which was certainly part of it, but rather because it would mean 10 more days of bed rest—10 more days before I could begin rehabilitation to get out of this hospital and be home with my family.

The plastic surgeon returned the next day to give his official assessment. He said the graft looked "awesome." Yes! He said that I could put weight on my leg (meaning I could resume normal rehab to try walking), and he also gave the official sign that I was now "medically cleared." Praise God!

After exactly 40 days and 40 nights of being in the hospital, I was now officially "medically cleared"—that is, I was declared free of infection and no longer needed heavy-duty antibiotics or medical intervention. All I needed to do was learn to walk again.

Chapter
Twenty-seven

First Steps to Going Home

Walking again wasn't easy. I completely underestimated the amount of time it would take for my rehabilitation. The main problem was that my left leg, because of the numerous surgeries and subsequent skin grafts, had been fixed in a slightly bent position (about 20 degrees, I'd say) for 40 days straight. Everything in that leg was ridiculously tight—muscles, tendons, ligaments—and there was a lot of swelling, which caused significant pain and discomfort. Initially I couldn't get my heel to touch the ground. The nice rehab people who had worked with me in the ICU also worked with me in the regular ward. With a lot of physical support, they had helped me to transition from a large walker to a normal walker to trying crutches in the ICU, before I was grounded again for the skin grafts. They were so kind, and we had a mutually great relationship—they had a patient who was unusually eager to push hard (often too hard, mind you!) so that he could get home to be with his family, and I had the pleasure of working with awesome gals with great senses of humour and attitude.

They were painful times for sure, but my body progressed rapidly (by this point did you expect any less?) and they recommended a transfer to a special rehabilitation centre in the city, called St. Michael's

Health Centre. The nurses and therapists at St. Michael's focused specifically on post-acute rehabilitation. "PARP" they called it—Post Acute Rehabilitation Program. Having been medically cleared, all we had to do was wait for a bed opening.

I was eager to get there as quickly as possible. Being in a place focused solely on rehabilitation meant that I was going to be able to get back to independence much more quickly and thus be able to go home with my wife and children. (You can tell that by now I was desperate to get home.) It was a Friday afternoon after being "medically cleared" when they put the official application in, meaning that as early as Monday I could possibly be transferred.

A Kiss from Heaven

One particular day of that weekend while I was waiting to be transferred was very memorable. I'd woken up wishing that I could get into a vehicle and someone could drive me to a place like Wendy's, say, for a burger! (I don't actually mind hospital food, but I just had a craving for a nice burger from Wendy's—what can I say?) I dismissed the thought as quickly as it had come because I'd already arranged to have lunch in the cafeteria with my friend Dr. Stephen Crawford, who, as a hospitalist, was now my attending doctor since I no longer needed the close attention of half a dozen specialists and our family physician was out of the country. *Mmmmm…cheeseburger,* I thought. *Ah well. One day.*

Bishop Todd came to visit that morning, and we hung out for about an hour, talking about things God had done in people's hearts and so forth, as well as just generally catching up. He suddenly randomly asked me if I'd like him to take me in the wheelchair for a walk outside around the hospital.

"Wow! That would be awesome!" I said. I had only been outside briefly once on a little "date" with my wife, but when we left the building, it was windy and cold (and I had lost my natural insulation), so she wheeled me right back up to my room. But it was beautifully pleasant that day in May, and the thought of feeling the warm sun on my face and breathing fresh air that hadn't been circulated through a filter—well, it sounded exactly like what I needed. I'd been cooped up for so long.

So, Todd wheeled me to the elevators, and as he wheeled me out again, Steve happened to be standing right there. He was about to begin his lunch break, so he joined us on our little walk!

Awesome—I get to hang out outside, with two of my amazing friends, in the bright sun, and the fresh air...How could this day get any better?!

After a leisurely stroll and stimulating conversation, we approached the entrance to go back inside. Just before we passed the entry to the staff parkade, Steve said something like, "We could go inside and eat our lunch in the cafeteria, or we could get into my vehicle and go to a drive-through or something...?"

"No way! Seriously?"

He smiled and nodded.

"Absolutely!!" I said.

On the way to his vehicle, he asked me where I wanted to go. It took no time to decide. "Let's go to Wendy's!" (To date, I have not received any coupons from Wendy's head office for this endorsement...hint, hint!)

We parked in front of a beautiful park, opened the sunroof, and ate our greasy, cheesy, and incredibly yummy burgers and fries. (No, Wendy's hasn't paid us to put their name in here or anything—I just enjoy food...and describing it apparently!) We watched the people go by on their bikes and roller blades, enjoying the beautiful, late-spring day.

It was as if God had given me a kiss. It felt so good to be alive and to be loved and known by the Creator Himself. It was just a fleeting thought in my mind that morning to eat a Wendy's burger—an impossible thought even—but He knows our desires and cares about even the most minute details of our lives. Sometimes we think He only cares about the big stuff—the stuff that *really* matters—but it's not true. He knows us intimately, and it *all* matters to Him. We're usually just too distracted to notice His kisses, although this one He made pretty obvious. And I was grateful. So grateful.

Financials

Speaking of kisses from heaven and being grateful, some of you may wonder how we made it financially during this time. First off, as a Canadian, my medical expenses were fully covered. One doctor estimated it might have cost about three to four million dollars for treatment during my entire hospital stay. It was nice not to have to worry about that, to say the least. Next, our employer, Heritage Christian Online School, was so good to our family. Not only did they take care of us financially, but the staff was incredibly supportive, immediately taking care of all of our teaching responsibilities until we were ready to return. Lara didn't have to worry about anything—they took care of it all. Finally, a number of people also helped us out during this time, graciously giving as their hearts desired.

What a blessing it is when you know that other people have your back—when you feel that you don't have to fight your battles alone. It was all so overwhelming (I cried many, many tears) and so wonderful to feel loved and supported by so many people on all levels. We truly didn't lack one thing during this time. We humbly praise God for every blessing and for every person He sent our way during that time and are eternally grateful.

Chapter
Twenty-eight

First Day at the Rehab Centre

Monday morning came, and wouldn't you believe it—good news! Apparently, there were three empty beds at St. Michael's, and they were going to transfer me that day already! I was overjoyed. But a few minutes later came some bad news. It was true that there were three empty beds, but they could only accommodate two new people in one day and I was third on the list.

Rats! That was a bummer, to be honest. I really wanted to get rehabbing sooner than later and get home! But I tried to get over it quickly by simply being thankful that I'd get in by Tuesday, which was still better than what I'd initially thought.

And then, about 30 minutes later, I was informed that the person second on the list wasn't ready to be moved yet and that I was to be transferred instead. *Yay!* I thought, *awesome!* (Though I did hope that the other person was okay, and I said a little prayer for them, whoever they were.) When the time came to transfer me, a nurse helped me into a wheelchair, loaded me up with my belongings in a couple of plastic bags, and placed the massive binder on my lap (think bigger than any binder you've ever seen). It had all my charts and stuff from the time of my entire hospitalization—it actually used to be two such large binders, but one nurse was able to simplify it and pack it all into just one massive binder. She wheeled me outside where one of those buses with a handicap lift took me over to St. Michael's. As the driver wheeled me up to the entrance, I figured the worst was over and now it was time to rehab so I could finally blow this joint and get me home!

Turns out, it was the *worst* day I'd had since my hospitalization. Well, the worst day that I can remember—I hear that Good Friday was pretty bad....

Longing to Be Home

My room in the rehab centre didn't look anything like the hospital rooms I'd been in. It was more like a small apartment, with homey furnishings, a nice wardrobe, a large window, and a separate bathroom. It was a welcome change, to be sure. The staff member giving me the orientation tour told me residents here were encouraged to be as autonomous as possible. It was an excellent system for motivating independence, since patients couldn't rely on nurses as much to do things for them like take them to the bathroom or help them dress, etc. St. Michael's also didn't have the regular foot traffic that a normal hospital location has. There was less noise from the public address system or banging food carts or urgent conversations in the hallway, but on that day, I could've used some distraction.

It had been building up for a while, my longing to be home, but that day it seemed to hit the hardest. I broke. Tears rolled down my face as I lay in my new bed, alone, crying out to God. *I want to be home...Please, God, I just want to be home.* I was missing my family so much. This little apartment-like room was more homey, but it still had sterile, impersonal hospital room aspects and was a reminder that this was not my home. I had been in the hospital for almost six weeks, and I wondered how the children's hearts were dealing with their dad being gone so long. I think I felt guilty for it all—that my kids were getting short-changed by not having their daddy there to encourage and help them. I know I shouldn't have felt guilty—it wasn't as if I did anything to bring this on—but it was how I felt inside. I wished this was all over and I was just home, where I should be.

Ordinarily I would have processed it with Lara that night when she came for her regular evening visit, but we had a family coming to stay at our house with us for a while and other friends had come to help them move some stuff in, so Lara spent time at home and hung out with the wives that night. I knew that it was good that she had some girl time, but I sure felt her absence.

Hospitals can be lonely. I had been fortunate to have so many friends and family come visit me regularly throughout the past weeks, so I didn't suffer that much; however, this rehab centre was probably the worst for loneliness, as there's not the usual traffic in and out of the room that might be in a usual ward. In the coming days, I spent so much time and effort concentrating on physiotherapy that there wasn't nearly the amount of time for visitors as before anyway. But that night, as it turned out, I had no visitors at all. It was just me and my tears and my heartache. It was a hard night—and unfortunately, it got worse.

Withdrawals

I had been on a very large dose fentanyl patch, a powerful narcotic painkiller, from the beginning of my hospitalization. It steadily delivered the narcotic and made it tolerable for my body to handle the pain of the disease, the surgeries, and subsequent recovery.

The doctor had steadily been lowering the fentanyl dosage throughout, but up to that point, I'd never noticed any withdrawal symptoms. My wife had though. She could see my hands shake, and the way I would sometimes anxiously ask for the next morphine dose. She saw the signs…and combined with stories she'd heard in the past, she was quite worried that when I would finally be discharged from the hospital, I would take with me an addiction to powerful painkillers. Concerned about this possibility, she actually told Bishop Todd about it, and he promised her that if that were the case when I left, he and a few others would take me to a cabin in the mountains, cold turkey, and stay with me until I was free. She relayed this conversation to me, and although I honestly wasn't worried about it at all up to that point, I fully agreed to it to make her happy. The truth was that of course I would be willing. I hate taking any kind of medicine anyway, and I don't want to be on it a day longer than absolutely necessary. I just didn't realize how badly I was already addicted to the painkillers at that point.

That day—the day they transferred me to the rehab facility—I was encouraged to try to drop a bit more significantly off of the patch, from a level of 50 (at one point I was at 200) down to zero. I was told that if it was more of a drop than my body could handle, then I could always go back up to 50 and go down more slowly. So, I took it off around nine in the morning before being transferred, but by early that evening, I began to experience symptoms. (In hindsight, it was possibly a contributing factor to my elevated emotions that night.)

I started to get cold…I pulled the blanket up to my neck and tried to get warm, and in 30 seconds I was warm again. But then, I was too warm. Hot in fact. I quickly pulled the blanket down to my waist. *That's better. Wait, I'm getting cold. Very cold. Quick! I need to pull the blanket up to my neck again.* Thirty seconds later I was hot again, so I pulled it barely down to my chest…cold again…

And that's how it went, all night. No matter what I tried, I just couldn't regulate my temperature. I asked the nurse to check me for anything unusual, but I didn't have a fever or anything. Then I remembered having taken off the patch and suddenly realized what was happening.

…Right…Wow…This sucks. I'm actually experiencing withdrawal symptoms. Crazy…I've never taken drugs in my life, and now this. Is this what withdrawals feel like? It must be what I'm going through.

It was extremely uncomfortable, to put it mildly. Always too hot or too cold, coming in wave after wave, and I couldn't sleep. I asked for a sleeping pill to try and help, but I think I still only got a couple hours of sleep that night. It was brutal, and in the morning, I spoke to the doctor about it. He agreed that it was likely withdrawal symptoms and said that it takes about 12 hours for much of the drug to wear out of your system, which explains why I had started feeling the symptoms then.

"How long could the symptoms last?" I asked.

"Well, it could take days, even weeks," he answered.

Weeks?! Now I was concerned. Here I was, on powerful narcotics, initially a necessary thing in my situation, but now my body seemed to have acquired a level of dependence on them. *Frustrating. Frustrating!*

Have you ever gone through a high point or breakthrough in your life only to have it immediately followed by another low point? Or in my case, two low points—missing my kids and painkiller addiction. Sometimes our journeys are very difficult, and we can feel like the Psalmist David did at times, with the competing emotions of successes and setbacks at the same time. All we can do is pray and ask for help and then trust in the kind of faithfulness God has shown to us in the past—it's always there if we sincerely look for it. We can trust Him to be the same now, which He always is, because He never changes.

Now I *really* wanted to get off of any drugs. I'd successfully gotten off morphine the week prior, and hadn't had any serious withdrawal symptoms then. (Mind you, my wife says there were lots! I just didn't notice.) But fentanyl was far more powerful, I found out later, and I was now about 24 hours into getting off it and the symptoms showed no signs of letting up. As much as I wanted to be free, it was too hard for me. *Why be a hero,* I reasoned, *when I can go off slowly?* Furthermore, the doctor had reminded me that I needed my body to be in a good state to be able to do all the physio prescribed for me. So, I took the doctor's advice to go back on the patch, though only at 25 this time. "Let's see if that's sufficient," he said, "And if not, we can do 37.5 or even 50 again for a bit if necessary."

In three hours, which is the amount of time it takes for the drug to work into your system, my body suddenly relaxed. It was fine again—but only because it had its chemicals. *Relief.* But I was still coming to terms with the fact that my body was addicted to painkillers, and I wasn't exactly thrilled about it. I was bent on getting this out of my system—although I finally respected the power of it, and now I understood Lara's earlier concerns. I'm now extremely sympathetic toward anyone addicted to any sort of drug, whether it's a recreational drug or prescribed painkiller. I realize that many, maybe even most, people who take drugs do so not necessarily because of how it makes them feel when they take it but rather because of how they will feel if they *don't* take it. Another lesson of compassion learned.

While He Lay Dying

It's amazing how God can use any and all situations to shape us, improve us, and bring about good. Indeed, it is my very favourite quality about God that He can turn things meant for evil into good, taking what is damaged and transforming it into something better than it ever was before (Genesis 50:20, Romans 8:28). Amazing—and I'll love Him forever for that quality alone.

Well, we kept the dosage constant for a few days at that level, and my body responded well. *Awesome!* Then we went down to 12.5, and then I came off entirely. I prayed each time that it would work and was also given some medication to help manage some of the symptoms. It was so much better this time. I experienced mild symptoms, if at all, and soon I was entirely off any narcotics. Hallelujah!

My brother-in-law was on staff at University Hospital in Edmonton, Alberta, where part of his job was working with people addicted to painkillers. When he called to check on my progress and heard that I was already off all the narcotics, he was surprised! Unknown to me, we had actually reduced the dosages faster than usual, and I had come off quite quickly compared to most patients. Cool! I'll chalk it up as, oh, miracle #26. I'm not sure how many answers to prayer there were in total to this point, but I bet it had to be up in the 20s or 30s by now!

First Actual Steps

They say that valleys in our lives are often followed by mountain top experiences, but after the hardest day so far, I was just happy to be out of the valley, with my tears dry and my withdrawal symptoms now subsiding. It turned out that my first official day of physiotherapy, on Tuesday, would take me back up the mountain again.

The physiotherapist came to my room to fetch me, and I wheeled myself down to the physio room in my newly fitted wheelchair that they'd taken some time to try and tailor fit for me, because of my height. Like pretty much everyone else I'd encountered, the physiotherapist was kind and understanding. She said we'd begin with a balance test to establish a baseline from which we could measure my progress. She then asked me to stand up and, without any walker or aid of any sort, do the first test: stand for one minute straight. Now, that may sound easy, but you have to realize that up to this point, my left heel still wasn't able to touch the ground when standing because everything was still so tight. Plus, all my muscles had atrophied so I was still weak and especially unbalanced.

I stood there as she started the clock...15 seconds...pretty good so far...30 seconds...getting harder...45 seconds...teetering, but almost there. *You can do it, Bruce,* I told myself, *you can do it.* Hold on...one minute! Whew! "Can I sit down?!"

She was impressed, as was I, and I tried to catch my breath.

More tests followed—move this way, bend that way, pick this up from the floor (we were both surprised I could do that one). This went on for about 10 to 15 minutes or so, but all the time something was happening that I never noticed. While I stood there, bending and moving, my left leg was slowly stretching out...

Suddenly, I realized that I was standing there with both feet flat on the ground! This was incredible! While walking with a walker in the hospital ward weeks prior, I would literally long for, even dream of the day when my leg would finally be stretched out and I could actually walk properly. In my mind, it was the only thing keeping me from being home! Once I could stretch my leg out, I just knew I would come home quickly afterwards. So, this day couldn't have come soon enough. And it was here, finally.

While the physiotherapist was nearby getting something else ready for the next exercise, I slowly moved my left foot forward slightly. *Feels good,* I thought. Then I moved the right one. Again, it felt good. Left, then right, slowly moving each foot inches ahead. I was walking! Well, more a kind of shuffling, really, but walking nonetheless.

"Look at this!" I said to her. "Check this out!!" I was so excited!

"Easy, Bruce!"

I shuffled some more, all without holding a walker or anything.

"Bruce, be careful! You probably shouldn't do that."

I started to shuffle a ways off this time, out of her reach unintentionally. It felt so amazing. I was walking!!

"Check this out! This is incredible!!" I exclaimed.

And then the physiotherapist actually got pretty upset at me! They don't want anyone to fall, and I totally understand that, of course. It was really quite foolish of me to go that far without any aid or way to stop a fall—but I just couldn't help it! I was walking!! I was walking!!! Though they were only little steps, for the first time in a month and a half, I was walking! I was walking on my own! I was walking!!!

Later that day when I had my first visitor (actually, for all the visitors I had that day!) I would get out of my bed and say, "Check out the new 'trick' I just learned!" and I'd show off my new moves, shuffling a few steps forwards. Haha…yeah, it was pretty fun. And people were completely shocked! Most had only ever seen me in bed with my leg elevated to reduce the swelling or at best seen me move awkwardly and with difficulty into my wheelchair to go to the bathroom with a nurse's assistance, so to see me swing my legs over the side of the bed and then proceed to stand up and then take steps?! They were amazed. And I would just smile, feeling so proud of myself. You would think I had just climbed Everest. Yeah, it was the best day I'd had since my hospitalization.

I actually told everyone who observed my performance to keep my little "trick" a secret. Bishop Todd, Dr. Steve, and I hatched a plot way back in the ICU for me to surprise everyone at church one Sunday once I was able. I thought it'd be extra fun if people didn't even know I could walk beforehand. Wouldn't they be surprised!

Discharge Date

The next day, physiotherapists, occupational therapists, recreational therapists, nurses, and a doctor stood around my bed. Every Wednesday was the weekly meeting where the staff would discuss with each patient how their progress was going and anything related to that, including, as in my case, the schedule for release! I was particularly eager to know how long I was going to have to be there, this final stage of my hospital journey.

The head nurse flipped some pages in my chart. "So…," she looked at a calendar on the wall, "we're looking at a discharge date…" she glanced down at the chart again, "and we're thinking May 30th."

"May 30th?" I was actually quite disappointed. "That long? Another three weeks?" Oh man, I just wanted to be home already. I had taken my first unassisted steps and everything!

"Is that date firm?" I asked.

"Not necessarily. That's our conservative estimate based on initial assessment, but we won't keep you in here any longer than you have to be."

It was probably meant to be an encouraging statement, but by this point in my hospitalization, I'd come to realize that medical personnel have their own med-speak. You'll never, ever hear them use the words "definitely" or "absolutely" and such, unless it's in a phrase like "definitely maybe" or "absolutely there's a chance." And so, I took her words to be a bit non-committal, with the subjective nature of assessing progress. However, I still saw it differently. I saw a bit of light that looked like hope. If anything my journey had taught me, it's that with God, nothing is impossible.

So, it could change, eh? I'll beat that by at least a week if not better, I thought. And that became my goal. *Two weeks or less and I'll be home...home again where I belong and where we'll be together as a family like we're supposed to be.*

The funny thing is when the doctor heard me relay that date, the first thing he thought, though he just kept it to himself at the time, was "He'll beat that."

And beat it I did. Every day I worked hard, very hard, pushing myself as far as the physiotherapist would allow. I thought to myself, *they really do know best and I'm going to listen to everything they say and rely heavily on their wisdom and experience, but as far as my body will allow, subject to their recommendations, I will push it.* On the next day of physio, I officially progressed from a walker to crutches, and by Friday, I was officially onto the cane. My progress was absolutely remarkable, and again, the physiotherapists were amazed and delighted.

One day a staff member admitted to me, "We have never seen anyone like you. It's hard to make predictions about what to expect. As far as I know, we have only ever had one other patient before who survived severe necrotizing fasciitis, but they were here to learn to cope with severe permanent disabilities. Your case is different. Very different."

Chapter Twenty-nine

⎯⩗⎯

Sleep

It's funny in life how we can experience amazing success and excitement in some areas of our lives and simultaneously experience setbacks and frustration in others. Most people didn't know this at the time, but my sleep patterns were entirely messed up. I guess sleeping for three weeks straight has a way of messing up your body clock—who knew? But now I could no longer manage to sleep normally at all. Every single night in the hospital, whether in the ICU, the main ward, or the rehab centre, I woke up after only 45 minutes or so of sleep. Sometimes I could sleep for an hour or maybe a bit longer, but that was rare. It would usually take about 15 minutes to half an hour until I could sink into sleep, and then sure enough, 45 minutes later I'd resurface. And this is how it went, all night long, day after day, and week after week. No matter what special sleeping pill or remedy I tried, prescription or otherwise, this was how I slept.

To be completely honest, I wasn't actually frustrated about it. It just was what it was. I think it really helped that I had so much to be thankful for—that's always powerful and I could talk a ton about that. But what I'd also do during the nights to help from getting frustrated about not sleeping—which is counterproductive, as anyone who has ever had sleep issues can understand—was that I would decide that I wasn't trying to sleep, per se, but rather that I was merely resting. If I fell asleep, it was a bonus. That, combined with thankfulness, seemed to do the trick, though it still didn't seem to fix my sleep issues, which persisted for many months.

Now as many people reading this will know, when you're awake at night, just lying there with nowhere to go and nothing to do, you often spend a lot of time thinking about things. You think about things that happened and the way they happened. You think about what you learned and how you have changed. You wonder about the effect events have had on others. In the still of the night, ponderings fill the long hours. I suppose the great thing about insomnia is that it affords you time to think.

During my 9 weeks in the hospital, many people, including my wife, who has no problem being honest with me, told me that I had a very good attitude throughout this whole ordeal. I hadn't really thought about it up to that point, but I suppose I did. I wondered why. I'm not special—I'm just like everyone else. Yet despite contracting flesh eating disease, suffering extreme pain at times, experiencing severe weakness from muscle atrophy, losing the ability to speak, going through drug withdrawal, as well coping with sleep issues, nerve damage and pain in my feet, and nausea, not to mention being away from my family for so long, I never seemed to ask the obvious questions:

"This is horrible and unfair—why did this happen to me?"

"This has been really hard—what did I do to deserve this?"

Or even perhaps: *"Why did I experience a miracle when some did not?"*

Although I can appreciate that people want to ask "why" questions, I have learned they're typically not that helpful. They're seldom answered and often lead to frustration, self-absorption or self-pity, and become a distraction from the more important questions of the moment:

"God, what are you doing in this now?"

"Lord, what would You like me to do now?"

For some reason, instead of being mired in why questions or grumbling and complaining, I seemed to be able to maintain a fairly positive attitude throughout. There had to be a reason why my attitude was like that. I thought about it, and I identified two truths that got into me early on in my Christian journey—truths that have affected how I perceive things.

The first of these is *thanksgiving.*

The Bible says "give thanks in all circumstances" (1 Thessalonians 5:18a). When you're thankful, there's not much room for grumbling and complaining. You can't dwell on what's going wrong, because in order to be truly thankful, your attention is directed toward the good things God has done and is doing. No matter how *bad* things get, there are always things to be *thankful* for. I was thankful for being alive, to be sure, but also for the awesome people I met in the hospital, for the friendships that deepened all over the place, for the multitude of lives that were touched through this, and for the way people's faith in God and in His desire to answer prayer was rejuvenated. There is always something to be thankful for. (And as my wife keenly points out, the same is true for the opposite, if we are not careful. No matter how *good* things are, we can always find something to *complain* about.)

The other truth that helped me have a good attitude—a very powerful truth indeed—was that I don't consider my life to be my own. It belongs to Jesus.

My car is not mine.

My house is not mine.

My money is not mine.

My wife is not mine.

And yes, even my body is not mine.

I merely consider these things to be entrusted to me. Jesus is the Master, and I'm the servant—a steward, if you will, of everything He gives me, so when I look at all that happened through this and all the many blessings that came to me and to other people—and this may be hard for some to believe—honestly, I would do it all again. It was worth it, by far.

I realize that this idea of our lives not being our own is foreign to our present culture. Ours is a culture that doesn't appreciate the idea of being under authority, and yet we are under authority every moment of our lives. From birth, we are under the authority of our parents, and as we grow up, we are under the authority of our teachers, the police, our government, etc. We are always under some kind of authority. It's inescapable. And the same is true spiritually.

The Bible says that those who trust in Jesus Christ as their Saviour have been transferred from a kingdom of darkness to the kingdom of God's beloved Son. In other words, no matter which side we're on— darkness or light—we're always in a kingdom and somebody is the king, the big boss—and it's not us. As Christians, Jesus is our King. And we belong to Him.

Here are a few verses that illustrate that very principle, that our lives—everything we have—belong to Jesus Christ:

> "So, my brothers and sisters, you also died to the law through the body of Christ, that you might belong to another, to him who was raised from the dead, in order that we might bear fruit for God" (Romans 7:4).

> "If we live, we live for the Lord; and if we die, we die for the Lord. So, whether we live or die, we belong to the Lord" (Romans 14:8).

> "Do you not know that your bodies are temples of the Holy Spirit, who is in you, whom you have received from God? You are not your own; you were bought at a price. Therefore honor God with your bodies" (1 Corinthians 6:19,20).

Of course, the great thing about this is that our King is entirely good, through and through. So instead of Him demanding submission from us, which He has every right to do (Romans 14:11 says that eventually everyone will bow their knees to Him), at present Jesus simply looks for those who willingly answer His call and say yes to Him— *"Yes, You gave everything You have for me. I now give everything I have to You."*

Jesus isn't asking us to do anything He didn't already do Himself. He gave everything He had to the Father—even at the most costly of times, saying the ultimate phrase of submission "Not my will, but yours be done" (Luke 22:42). Consider the words penned about His life by the Apostle Paul to the church in Philippi:

> "Who, being in very nature God, did not consider equality with God something to be used to his own advantage; rather, He

made himself nothing by taking the very nature of a servant, being made in human likeness. And being found in appearance as a man, He humbled himself by becoming obedient to death—even death on a cross!" (Philippians 2:6-8).

He became obedient even to the point of death. It really does cost to follow God. And there's sometimes sadness and grieving in that, in terms of how much we will have to give up. The truth is, to fully be a disciple of Jesus *will* cost us everything. Jesus doesn't ask for half of our heart; He asks for it all. But there is good news in that. When we deny ourselves and lay down our lives—the meagre amount we have to offer anyway in comparison—we actually *gain* everything!

"For whoever wants to save their life will lose it, but whoever loses their life for me will find it" (Matthew 16:25; see also Mark 8:35, Luke 9:24).

"Therefore I tell you, do not worry about your life, what you will eat or drink; or about your body, what you will wear. Is not life more than food, and the body more than clothes? Look at the birds of the air; they do not sow or reap or store away in barns, and yet your heavenly Father feeds them. Are you not much more valuable than they? Can any one of you by worrying add a single hour to your life? "And why do you worry about clothes? See how the flowers of the field grow. They do not labor or spin. Yet I tell you that not even Solomon in all his splendor was dressed like one of these. If that is how God clothes the grass of the field, which is here today and tomorrow is thrown into the fire, will he not much more clothe you—you of little faith? So do not worry, saying, 'What shall we eat?' or 'What shall we drink?' or 'What shall we wear?' For the pagans run after all these things, and your heavenly Father knows that you need them. But seek first his kingdom and his righteousness, and all these things will be given to you as well" (Matthew 6:25-33).

I'm not exactly sure how, but through all of this He somehow got more of my heart and He has more possession of me. And as strange as it may sound, although I feel the most constrained and bound to the Lord I have ever felt, instead of feeling like more of a slave, I actually feel the most free that I've felt in my entire life. I can't explain it. I'm not sure how it happened—but somehow, Jesus got more of me. And I love it.

Indeed, it seems that to the degree to which Jesus is Lord in our lives is the degree to which we will live a fruitful—and happy I might add—Christian life. Now the good news is this: only the Holy Spirit can produce a heart of holiness or separation to God (sanctification). After all, He is called "the Spirit of Holiness" (Romans 1:4). Consider such precious promises:

> "He who began a good work in you will carry it on to completion until the day of Christ Jesus" (Philippians 1:6b).

> "May God himself, the God of peace, sanctify you through and through. May your whole spirit, soul and body be kept blameless at the coming of our Lord Jesus Christ. The one who calls you is faithful, and he will do it" (1 Thessalonians 5:23,24).

We cannot make ourselves more holy. Believe me, I tried. In fact, if anyone tried in life, boy, how I tried (that's a whole story in itself). No, God is the One who sanctifies and makes us holy.

See, one of the coolest parts in this ordeal is that arguably one of the greatest accomplishments of my life, one that affected tens of thousands of lives all over the world, was accomplished by simply resting on that hospital bed.

Doing nothing.

At all.

What a beautiful picture there: if we just lay down our lives...our rights...and we say, "Anything for You, Jesus," He will do the rest. He will change us, and the world, through our simple act of trust and submission.

I obviously can't take any credit for what happened—after all, it wasn't exactly something I volunteered for! Perhaps the only thing I did that one could argue opened the door for God to use something like this for His glory was praying a specific prayer—one that I've prayed all my life, sometimes every day for years: *Lord, do anything You have to do to get me where You want me to be.*

It's kind of a blank cheque, and it gets results.

If we're willing, God can use even the darkest hours of our lives and the fiercest attacks of evil to further His kingdom and His good purposes. If we really want Him to be the Lord of our lives and to give Him full control of our lives, some things may happen to us that are uncomfortable, but through it all He will intentionally and deliberately use them to further His purposes in our lives and others' lives. For example, at one point Jesus tells the disciple Peter, formerly called Simon, that "Satan has desired to sift all of you as wheat. But I have prayed for you, Simon, that your faith may not fail. And when you have turned back...strengthen your brothers" (Luke 22:31,32).

In other words, although there was going to be an outright evil, demonic attack upon Peter's life, Jesus didn't say He'd stop it immediately or shield Peter entirely from it. But rather, He prayed that his faith would be strong in it—not just so that Peter would be able to stand up against it and not fail, but also so that afterwards he could help other people who are also struggling.

It gives an interesting insight into why Jesus now lives to continually make intercession for us (Hebrews 7:25). It would seem that Christ, our Victor, is praying for us, so that when the trials come that challenge our faith, we will be able to stand strong and face whatever comes at us and to grow as a result of it.

Please don't read me wrong: I'm not speaking fatalistically that every bad thing comes from the hand of God. I don't believe that at all. Jesus said that there is a devil, the enemy of our souls, and he lives to steal, kill, and destroy (John 10:10). But there is also One who will turn around the devil's attacks to further His purposes (Romans 8:28).

Consider the stories of Peter, as mentioned, and Job or Joseph. Not only can God turn bad things into good stories, he can use bad things to actually accomplish His intended purposes. He plays both sides of the chessboard. It's almost like a trap that the devil falls into, like when he incited the Jews to kill Jesus. It ended up resulting in the salvation of the world, no less! In my case, though the devil tried to kill me, through it God raised up an army to pray for me. As a result, He strengthened people's faith, highlighted the power and need for community, especially in crisis, and once again reminded so many people of the power of unified prayer to our God and Father, and much more. In the devil's desire to thwart the plans of God by snuffing out a flame, he ended up sparking a forest fire.

Anyway, those are some of the thoughts I had in the still of the night.

More Sleep

My sleeplessness persisted, long after I got out of the hospital in fact. It wasn't until many months after my official discharge, sitting around an outdoor fire pit with a bunch of good buddies, talking about life and sharing stories, when my sleep breakthrough finally began to come. I was sitting there listening to someone talk about how recently he had just gone through a two-year bout with severe insomnia and how it was beginning to destroy his life. He would fall asleep at red lights, be increasingly disagreeable at home, and not function well at work. Something had to change, and eventually he went to get prayer from a couple pastors after church one Sunday.

They prayed with him and recommended that he and his wife pray through their home as well, just to make sure there wasn't anything in there that was inadvertently or overtly in opposition to God perhaps. And while doing that, they felt something evil in an upstairs room. When they'd originally moved into the house and were renovating, they'd found some old adult magazines stuffed behind a vanity unit, hidden away by the previous owner. They had gotten rid of the magazines as soon as they'd found them, but they now felt that they should linger in that room and pray there until it felt clean. After doing that and praying through the entire house, he tried it—he went to bed. For the first night in two years, he slept through the entire night, and then again the next night, and the next. Overnight, literally, his sleep issues were fixed.

While listening to his story, I realized something—I had received prayer for almost every other physical issue during my ordeal and had experienced God do miracle after miracle after miracle, both while I was asleep and after. But I'd never actually asked anyone to pray for my sleep! I guess I thought that since it wasn't causing frustration, why bother anybody with it? I hoped it would just improve eventually. But that's stupid logic really—why *not* ask for help? It was a bit of a risk, I guess. I had in my pocket the first of seven new prescription pills to be taken daily over a week period. The doctor thought it might help reset my sleep clock. But I wanted to give God a chance. So, I kept the pill in my pocket and asked the guys to pray for me. A number of them had encouragements from God for me, and one of them felt that it would gradually unfold for me, just like everything else had so far. Another guy saw me running again and felt that it would be a sign of my completed healing. It was all so encouraging. With hope in my heart, I went home to sleep.

The next night I had a couple two-and-a-half hour stretches of sleep, which were the longest I'd had in a long, long time. The next night and every night thereafter, my sleep improved—whether by sleeping in longer stretches or taking shorter times to fall sleep again, it slowly got better and better. Without any pills or medication, eventually I began to sleep the whole night through just like I had before. Praise God indeed! Miracle #45 or so?!

Chapter Thirty

Home for the Day

Anyway, back to the rehab centre. One of the coolest parts of my progress was when medical experts changed their minds about something. I initially found out there was a possibility that the physio could recommend I get a pass to visit home for a day. Consistent with my character, I brought it up right away—but I was immediately told that it probably wasn't safe and hence not realistic. Our house has a lot of stairs and little ones running about, and a fall could set back my progress, or even put a dent in it. The following week, when I brought up the topic again, the physio acknowledged a day pass was a "definite possibility." (Notice the med-speak again, ha-ha.) By Thursday, they had fully changed their minds based on seeing my progress and began to arrange for me to have a day pass that coming weekend.

And so, on Saturday, May 11th, exactly 50 days after having been admitted to the hospital, Lara picked me up in the van, and I came home. I simply can't express how overwhelming it was to step through the front door of my house, walk up the stairs by myself, hug my children on the sofa, and just be with my wife in our own home. I pretty much cried the whole day, at the drop of a hat.

While He Lay Dying

Lara's brother and family came down from High River to visit for the day. We kept my day pass a secret, so they were not expecting what came next. Chris and Shellie had rushed down on "Dark Friday" when it looked like I would not live. Chris found someone to take over his role as pastor in their church on Good Friday and Easter Sunday and they both took vacation time to stay the following week to help with the children. They helped with running the house and making practical repairs around the place and also joined the people praying in the hospital. Their daughter, Arianna, formed a strong bond with her baby cousin, Vivia, and doted on her like a living doll. Their son, Kaiden, became a source of entertainment for the other two. Arianna and Kaiden saw the crowds of people in the hallway of the hospital praying, and overheard the conversations in the house as people brought home daily reports. They had seen their parents go on a seven kilometre prayer walk every day, and they had prayed for me themselves. They heard the people in their home church praying for their uncle. Now here the family was just over a month later, all sitting in the kitchen together, playing with the kids, and asking Lara about my progress when I came around the corner and stood in the entrance to the kitchen.

"Hey, Bro!!" Chris said, jumping up to give me a hug. Shellie beamed. Their kids just stared at me, wide-eyed. They were so surprised to see me at home, they didn't know what to say. It was great seeing them all—I felt so much love for them and they for me.

At dinner, I remember them asking if I would give thanks for the food. It was the strangest thing, looking into everyone's eyes. My brother-in-law and his wife looked elated and moved to see me, yet my niece and nephew looked at me differently. They were staring in amazement at the answer to everyone's prayers, including their own.

We all sat in silence and bowed our heads to pray, and with Lara beside me squeezing my hand, I choked up. Finally, finally I mustered the only words I could squeeze out. "Thanks...God...Amen," which was followed by a flood of tears.

It was the happiest day I'd had since my hospitalization, and my heart was bursting with love and thankfulness to God! In fact, the day was so good, Lara and I thought we'd do it again the next day! Mother's Day! Yeah, as you can imagine, pretty much every special holiday like Mother's Day and Father's Day and Christmas are extra special now and will never, ever be the same again. Each one will be a precious gift to both of us and to our children. I can't help but swell with gratitude whenever I think about that.

Surprise Church Visit

Well, it was time! It was one week later—Sunday—and things were going awesome. I was progressing rapidly; now I kind of held my cane in my hand for a just-in-case moment—or for self-defense if needed! Given my progress, without me even bringing it up, the medical team at St. Michael's rehab hospital bumped my official discharge date up by one week to May 23rd, exactly two months to the day from when I was admitted.

My progress was "stunning—without exaggeration," the doctor said, and I had to admit, I was feeling marvellous. Each day I leapt forward in my ability to do things, whether it was how long I could sit or stand or how far I could walk or my stamina or general health energy-wise. I continually amazed people when they'd see me. My colour was returning, I was steadily gaining weight, and everyone said I was just looking better and better every time they saw me.

And now, it was time to go to church!

We had it all figured out. A few days before, my two great friends Stephen Barbour and Amos Martel were ordained as deacons in a special service. Not wanting to be a distraction, yet dearly wanting to be there for them, we stealthily snuck in, watched from an office at the back, and then snuck out again. Only a couple of people saw us—and they were sworn to secrecy. We decided to go to church on Sunday the same way. Lara and I would arrive at church fashionably late and hide out in Todd's office until he called us up.

A few minutes into his sermon, speaking about miracles, we heard our cue: "...but I thought, who better to talk about miracles than a walking, talking miracle himself."

While He Lay Dying

Holding hands, Lara and I emerged from his office at the back of the sanctuary and walked up to the front to shouts and clapping and crying and praise to God—the air in the church was electric with excitement! We got to share about how God still does miracles today. Lara had to get me some tissue as I thanked our God and our church family and commended them for their faith, love, and example. What amazing brothers and sisters in Christ we have! What an amazing church we belong to! But much more, what an amazing God we have!

If you'd like to watch the video clip of this yourself, you can find the link on the book's website located at the back of the book.

Home

On May 23rd, at 10:00 in the morning—exactly two months to the day and to the hour from when I initially went into hospital—I was officially discharged. Lara came to pick me up, and we loaded into our van. I was pretty excited, as you can imagine.

I'm going home...

It was a great day. It stands, without question, as one of the best days of my life.

Later that afternoon, when the kids were down for their nap and I was lying on the couch getting ready to begin reading all of the emails and Facebook messages I'd been sent, I decided to update my Facebook status. It was the first post I'd made since my ordeal began, and it simply read: *"It's great to be home."*

One of my friends quickly replied, *"Best post of the year!"*

I had to agree.

Part Three

A Broader Perspective

Chapter
Thirty-one

A Daughter's Take

"I think the reason God healed my daddy is because He knows we like to jump on him."

Keziah Merz, age four

Chapter Thirty-Two

‑╱╲╱╲‑

A Doctor's Take (Dr. Stephen Crawford)

"The whole hospital was overrun with gangrene...the face of the sufferer assumed a ghastly, anxious appearance...the slightest change in posture or the most delicate examination of the sore put [the patient] to torture...the bravest soldier betrayed the greatest imaginable impatience of pain and depression of spirits. Men who had borne amputation without a groan, shrank at the washing of the sores...sinking into sullen despair...the limb became horribly foetid...[it was] one of the most subtle and destructive poisons that ever infested an hospital, attacking equally the most robust and debilitated, and, if unchecked by medical aid, proceeding invariable to a fatal termination."

—John Hennen, surgeon during the Napoleonic wars
of 1803-1815, describing what is now widely believed
to have been necrotizing fasciitis or "flesh eating disease."

March 23, 2013. The text read, "This is Lara. Are you at the hospital today? Bruce is being admitted."

I wasn't "in house" at the time, having worked the night shift the night before, and I was just heading into the cinema with my kids. She filled me in with what they knew so far—"hamstring infected or something" "fluid on his muscle" "BP super low." It didn't sound great, but, I thought, Bruce is a big healthy guy, and the eternal optimist in me said, "he'll be alright." I sent up a prayer and honestly don't remember much of the movie because the cogs were slowly turning as I pondered what was going on with my friend. The next few texts from Lara were just before he went into his first surgery, and it rapidly became clear that this was something pretty nasty. His kidneys were under a lot of strain, and he was clearly in a state of septic shock—unable to keep his own blood pressure up, which in turn deprived his vital organs of the blood supply and therefore oxygen and nutrients they needed to function properly.

As a "hospitalist"—basically a family physician who sees patients who are in the hospital—one of the things that I spend a lot of my time doing is explaining what is going on to patients and families, translating from med-speak to English. That's what I tried to do for Lara from that first night and for the praying hordes in the ICU waiting room as time went on. Hopefully I can try to do the same for you as well and shed some light on what was going on in Bruce's body.

The bacteria that caused all this trouble started in Bruce's throat with a common complaint known as strep throat or streptococcal pharyngitis. For most people who pick up this bug, it means a few days of difficulty swallowing chips and cornflakes, feeling a bit under the weather. Some need a course of antibiotics to make it go away. Severity of infection, however, like buying or selling real estate, is all about location, location, location. The same bacteria, depending on location, can cause anything from strep throat to scarlet fever to rheumatic fever to necrotizing fasciitis. The real problems for Bruce came when this bug entered his bloodstream and took a ride to his thigh where it found a new home between layers of muscle, in a thin layer of tissue that separates the hamstring muscles, called fascia. Once there, the bacteria set to work, causing havoc with the blood vessels under his skin, leading to small clots, which plugged up those blood vessels and therefore interrupted the supply feed to the tissues downstream. When that tissue is starved of a blood supply, it causes cell death—also known as necrosis. The necrosis, along with the infection itself, causes swelling, which in turn causes pain. In med-speak, swelling is "itis." Joint swelling is arthritis, tonsil swelling is tonsillitis, swelling of the pancreas is pancreatitis...you can see where we're heading, right? Necrosis of the fascia causing swelling is necrotizing fasciitis. Maybe flesh-eating disease is easier?

It's likely that the particular strain of streptococcus that chose to make an appetizer of Bruce had an added sting in the tail—a protein called a superantigen attached to it, which set off a hugely complex chain of events that led to streptococcal toxic shock syndrome. In essence, this superantigen enabled a breeding family of bacteria in his leg to have a toxic effect on Bruce's kidneys, major blood vessels, and even his blood. At this stage it wasn't just eating his flesh, it had moved onto the main course of Bruce and kidney pie. More of a super *villain* than a superhero, this superantigen.

Throughout the course of Bruce's illness, there were many times where he could or even *should* have died.

Good Friday was the worst of times without a doubt, and any one of the myriad things that went awry inside of Bruce that day could easily have taken him from us, particularly the almost catastrophic bleed in his lungs. Had the situation been different, had a specialist with a different skill set been on duty that day for example, things could have turned out very differently.

But it was far from the only time his life was in danger. In the early stages of his admission, his blood pressure was so low that vital organs were failing and his body was unable to make any effort to maintain a healthy pressure.

His kidneys were failing and without dialysis were unable to perform their proper function. The infection could have spread further, as it frequently does, and that alone could have finished him off. The toxic shock is also a natural born killer; the low platelets contributing to a catastrophic bleed in another major organ or an open wound; the pneumonia that he developed while on the ventilator; the strain on his heart that was rattling along at roughly twice its resting rate for most of the time he was in the ICU—any or all of these could have made for a much shorter book.

So, by my count, there were at least six deadly processes at work in Bruce's body that would, could, and maybe even should have finished him off.

While He Lay Dying

I switched from being a family doctor splitting my time between a clinic and the hospital to working as a hospitalist in 2010. My office in the hospital is a few yards from the ICU, and in the three years I had been working there full time I had never seen the hallway so busy, and mostly with people I knew from church or was getting to know, as they were related to Bruce in some way. I was immensely proud of my medical, nursing, and managerial colleagues as I watched them deal courteously and professionally with this unprecedented situation as well as the fantastic treatment they provided in that ICU room for Bruce himself.

So Bruce left the hospital in a pale green minivan instead of a black hearse, accompanied by tears of joy (mine included) instead of tears of grief. The big question is, was this a miracle or a medical marvel? Was it the exceptional treatment that pulled Bruce back from the brink, or was there a divine hand at work?

I will come to a direct and definitive answer to that question, but first, a bit of background.

As a physician who has practiced in four countries on three continents over 14 years; as a junior doctor working in a variety of specialties from psychiatry to gynaecology, otolaryngology to orthopaedic surgery; as a busy family doctor in the UK and Canada and more recently as a hospitalist, I have a broad, if not super-specialized medical experience. I have dealt with a lot of very sick people, I've performed an amputation, I've watched people breathe their last—I've seen my fair share of death and suffering.

I also know Jesus Christ as my Saviour and Lord and His Father as Creator. It is humbling to understand even a little of the phenomenal intricacies of how our bodies are put together, how they tick, how the systems function together, and how they heal from injury or infection.

"Miracle," though, is a tricky and loaded word in the medical community. A lot of our work depends on our patients trusting our skill, our knowledge, and the science behind the treatments we prescribe. We treat whomsoever graces the doors of our clinics or hospitals—rich or poor, fat or fit, God-fearing or atheistic, those who are sick through no fault of their own and those who by design or neglect have caused their own sickness. In general, they come to us for our tangible medical knowledge and treatment, not for our intangible prayers. We also live in a society where in the minds of many, a Christian faith is tantamount to bigotry and has no place in the environment of a hospital or clinic. All of this was in the back of my mind as I prayed for Bruce during his admission.

There seems to be a natural stand-off between the supernatural and the scientific, but I believe it is largely a modern invention. There are many pioneering scientists of centuries past and present who, like me, find or have found ourselves operating in both. The way one approaches each is affected by the other. So I find, for instance, in my personal faith, I have always had an inquiring mind, and since I was a teenager, I was unwilling to simply take the claims of the Bible at face value without looking deeper for supporting evidence. Likewise, in my practice of medicine, I bring what my faith has taught me: a God-given love for my neighbour and a desire to serve, comfort, and heal—and a belief in miracles. This certainly wasn't the first time I've ever prayed for a miracle, and I had always had a healthy skepticism when I had heard about miracles happening. But I had never before seen something defy all scientific predictions on a scale like this.

In Bruce's case, I had complete confidence that the treatment of my medical colleagues was both comprehensive and appropriate. But I also understood the gravitas of the situation, and I wrestled with my respect for the disease, my medical experience, and my faith in praying for and believing for a miracle.

Unfortunately I have seen necrotizing fasciitis and other serious infections ravage people's bodies. Some survive, typically with life-altering repercussions, but never once have I seen them survive in anything approaching the nature of Bruce's survival and recovery or the amazing shape that he is in now. Usually such individuals are left with significant disabilities, physical or mental or both. Now more than a year after his discharge, all that Bruce has to show from his life-threatening ordeal is a little remaining nerve damage in his feet, a side effect of some of the medication he was given, and a couple of skin grafts. In stark contrast to my previous experience, the following is what I witnessed during Bruce's admission and beyond.

While He Lay Dying

1. Expectations shattered.

Early in Bruce's stay as the nurses watched his blood pressure rise along with the prayers at his bedside and in the waiting room, the unexpected was happening.

Later, as colour and life-giving blood returned before the eyes of those stood at the end of his bed to his corpse-like feet and the very fact that he survived without the loss of a single toe, never mind a limb or two, defied explanation.

In discussions I was present for, after the worst was past, the nephrology (kidney) specialist fully anticipated that Bruce would likely need months of ongoing dialysis. He needed none after that day—not just a bit more, or once a week, once a month—nothing. His creatinine level improved so rapidly that there was just no need.

On Good Friday as the medical team worked on Bruce, their expectations, based on many, many years of cumulative experience and knowledge, were that he was not going to make it. Don't get me wrong, I do not believe for a moment that that meant they weren't doing their utmost to change that, but it seemed hopeless in the ICU room. Yet, in the waiting room, the mood may have been sombre at times especially that day, but it never lacked hope.

The speed of his recovery was phenomenal. Partly this is due to excellent care and the great nurses, physiotherapists, and occupational therapists at the rehab unit. Partly it's that stubborn streak (actually it's more like a stubborn flood) that Bruce has. But all were flabbergasted by how quickly he got to his feet and walked out of that place. As I chatted one day to one of the nurses there who I used to work with, I had to assure her that, yes, this was the guy who'd had necrotizing fasciitis, and yes, he nearly died. She then showed me a picture pinned on the notice board in the rehab unit of the only other person she knew of who had been through their unit having survived necrotizing fasciitis. This amazing lady had tragically suffered facial disfigurement, lost both legs, her left forearm and fingers on her right hand, but was pictured swinging a golf club. Unfortunately, this (or worse) is viewed as the expected outcome of this aggressive disease.

2. Full healing and restoration.

In one of my texts in reply to Lara on the day Bruce was admitted, I wrote, "Hopefully the only thing he'll be left with is the scar and the story." Amazingly, despite everything, that's exactly how he left the hospital: he has a few scars and his life and limbs are fully intact. And *this* is the story. The Bruce I had lunch with the other day is physically, cognitively the same Bruce as before, less a few pounds that I and a few of his other friends are secretly a little jealous of.

3. A willingness and openness in Lara and Bruce's wider family to allow the world in to their pain and suffering in a beautiful and healthy way.

4. The Body of Christ (1 Corinthians 12) uniting in biblical proportions to pray fervently and without ceasing for one man.

So, I promised a straight answer: miracle or medical marvel? In fact, I will leave the final word to the internal medicine physician who dealt with the mayhem that was Good Friday 2013 in the Chinook Regional Hospital ICU. He approached me a few weeks after Bruce left the ICU and asked me how he was doing. I assured him Bruce Merz was doing remarkably well. His reply, with which I had to concur:

"You know, that that man is alive is nothing short of a miracle."

Chapter Thirty-Three

A Bishop's Take (Bishop Todd Atkinson)

The last thing Bruce said to me before being taken into surgery was, *"Todd, I am not afraid."* Still, I loved this man dearly and I didn't like seeing those heavy metal doors close behind him.

I had received text messages from both Bruce and Lara on that Saturday in March. The first message, from Bruce, was to let me know they would have to cancel the dedication ceremony for their baby the next day. He was suffering from what he described as an "utterly debilitating flu."

Lara sent the next texts informing me he was going to the hospital. He was in extreme pain from what doctors thought was a blood clot or a muscle infection. Her last text read, "He is just being admitted to the ICU. Dr. says it is quite serious." I left for the hospital.

I was taken immediately into Bruce's room in the Intensive Care Unit because he wanted to see me. We had a good time together talking and laughing. I assured him I wouldn't leave but would stay and pray for him throughout the surgery. When he came back, heavily sedated after the two-hour procedure, Lara and I were glad to hear the news that the infection was in a "pouch" and there appeared to be no major tissue damage. Just after 10:00 pm, I left Lara to go home. It seemed Bruce was in stable condition.

While He Lay Dying

It had been an unusual week as I tried to prepare for the Palm Sunday service. In the nine-and-a-half years I had been at River of Life Church, I always knew what God wanted me to preach. This week heaven seemed silent. I soon learned why. I did not in fact preach that Sunday. As our 10:30 am Sunday service was starting, I received an alarming notice from Lara that Bruce was crashing. I left the service straightaway for the hospital. We did a prayer vigil at Bruce's bedside for the next 23 hours, which was the first stint in the next 21 days of prayer.

From the start of this vigil, I felt this was not going to be a battle quickly won. I thought of the Old Testament prophet Daniel prevailing in prayer for 21 days until a breakthrough occurred. Romans 5:2-4 was also brought to my attention:

> "We rejoice in the hope of the glory of God. Not only so, but we also rejoice in our sufferings, because we know that suffering produces perseverance; perseverance, character; and character, hope. And hope does not disappoint us, because God has poured out his love into our hearts by the Holy Spirit."

From this I knew intuitively what Bruce's suffering would require of us who loved him. It would require perseverance. We would have to stand fast in faith and prayer.

For many of us, perseverance is not a spiritual quality that we aspire to. We seem rather to think that faith is evidenced by quick results. We get faith for something and start believing with the force of a steam train, but if we don't see the results we want, and quickly, we lose heart.

I think it may be more accurate to say we lose faith quickly because we have already lost heart. Losing faith is merely a symptom. Much like chest pain is a sign of a heart attack, so lack of perseverance is a sign that our heart has been damaged. Somewhere, somehow, the heart of the Canadian church has been deeply hurt, and this has made it hard for us to fully trust God like we dearly desire to.

However, now God had our attention. Someone's life was hanging in the balance, someone we loved deeply. Oh, thank God for love! God's love had been poured into our hearts. He caused us to love Bruce with a love that would rise to the occasion. Out of love we gathered around this family and prayed.

I don't think this would have happened if the people of River of Life Church hadn't dared to love deeply. You can turn love off like a valve, because it hurts to love, and many people do. But our congregation—they didn't shut it off. They actually opened up the valve. They let themselves love largely.

I'm also relieved we didn't have a form of Christianity that lacked a theology of suffering. Otherwise we would not have been able to hear what God wanted to say. If we didn't believe that God could work His good will even through suffering and bring forth resurrection on the other side of pain, we would have missed it and our faith would have been shot down early.

One of the initial things that God wanted to say to us through this trial was that He desired to work something *into* us; something that would enable us to hold the course. Human tendency is to want quick results, but it is only through perseverance that the character of Christ can be produced in us. That's why this trial *had* to take some time. Character formation does not take place quickly. This story was not merely about God wanting to change Bruce's condition; it was and is about God wanting to change our character.

Furthermore, "character produces hope." I felt that in the instance of Bruce's sufferings, God would work to produce true hope in us, the kind of hope "that does not disappoint." That was it! The heart of the Canadian church was suffering from a kind of crippled hope called disappointment. Perhaps we have been sold false hopes rather than true Biblical hope. False hope eschews suffering; it thinks of perseverance as merely an excuse for weak faith (because, it is supposed, strong faith would produce instantaneous results). False hope values charisma over character and in the end sets us up for deep heart-rending disappointment. But true God-given hope does not disappoint.

Admittedly, I have had an uneasy relationship with Romans 5:2-4. Is it really true that suffering produces perseverance, which produces character, which produces hope? In other words, do sufferings end in hope? Do I feel like my own sufferings have ended this way—in a net increase of hope?

Thus I knew from this first hour of prayer, a little of what we would all gain through "Bruce's story." On the other side of this we will have learned something about the value of perseverance, we will have Christ's character worked more deeply into us, and a measure of genuine hope will have been restored to our hearts. Emboldened by this promise, I hunkered down. The battle had only begun.

It's important to note that we were not fighting for Bruce's life because we were afraid of death. As Bruce confessed from the beginning, "Todd, I am not afraid." Death was once our taskmaster but now it is our servant! Because of Jesus' victory over death at the cross, death has been humbled. It cannot take us whenever it wishes. It has no final word. And it holds no terror for us. At the time of the Father's choosing, when He calls us to Himself, death is merely a doorman. It opens the door and allows us to pass from this life to the life to come. That is all. Which is why we can sing, "Oh grave, where is your victory? Oh death where is your sting?" (1 Corinthians 15:55).

That is why we neither fear death nor think that every time someone dies it must have been due to our failure. We take comfort knowing that even Jesus Himself laid down His life at the age of only 33 and thereby gained our salvation.

Premature death, however, is a different case. This time we strongly discerned, along with many others, that it was not Bruce's time to die. This life-threatening illness was a direct challenge to the will of God; and the church of God here in Lethbridge, across the country, and even across the world put their foot down and said, "This man shall not die. He shall live!" and then prayed in a persevering and selfless way.

When the stakes are high, you have to dig deep and discover what God has put within you. Years ago a friend did me the great favour of teaching me something invaluable about St. Paul's apostolic calling. He pointed out to me that St. Paul's New Testament letters were written in response to the challenges in the first churches. It was in having to address these challenges that St. Paul had to dig deep and found the Holy Spirit had already placed the resources he needed there. There was apostolic wisdom residing in him, but it required an external pressure to bring it out of him. This situation with Bruce was very much like that.

As day turned into night on Sunday, we were still at Bruce's bedside praying. I felt so terribly weak! Not just physically, but I felt weak in knowing how to pray in a way that would make a difference. This night

Romans 8:26 was more real to me than it had ever been: "the Spirit helps us in our weakness. For we do not know what to pray for as we ought" (ESV). I brought this to the attention of those in the room: Stephen, Amos, and Mark, Bruce's brother, who had just arrived from B.C. We prayed together saying, "God, we do not know how to pray! We ask that Your Holy Spirit would show us how we ought to pray!"

Within minutes the atmosphere in that room changed noticeably. The Holy Spirit was there! He was opening our eyes to see things we could not have otherwise seen, things that would inform us how we ought to pray. We began to perceive that there was more going on than meets the eye.

I could see that God had a national calling upon Bruce and that even *through* this infirmity, God had things to say to the nation of Canada. I could see those instances in Holy Scripture where a man's body acted like a prophetic signpost for a nation or nations (Isaiah 20:3; Ezekiel 4:4) and that this was now happening in Bruce's body. In some significant ways, Bruce's body was a prophetic signpost to the condition of the Body of Christ in our nation.

Bruce is an amazing man. He is large, strong, intelligent, and hugely capable. And yet here he lay unconscious due to an unwelcomed infection. This became a startling picture to us of the Body of Christ in our nation. The Church in Canada has vast potential but it is only living in a fraction of that potential. As we prayed, we wondered what the "infection" was that had immobilized the Body of Christ in Canada. We were drawn to Psalm 133: "Behold, how good and pleasant it is when brothers dwell together in unity! It is like the precious oil on the head, running down on the beard, on the beard of Aaron...It is like the dew of Hermon, which falls on the mountains of Zion! For there the LORD has commanded his blessing, life forevermore." Within minutes we began to receive text messages from people outside of the hospital who were interceding for Bruce. As they were praying, they also felt directed to Psalm 133—altogether unaware of what we were praying!

It suddenly seemed so self-evident to us! The Body of Christ is called to fulfill a substantial role within the nation, but disunity has prevented us from fulfilling our full potential. Division has kept the Body from functioning as it should. Unity is "good" and "pleasant" to the

Lord, and where He sees true unity He will "command his blessing, life forevermore."

It was significant to us that Bruce's brother Mark was in the room as this was happening. Bruce and Mark loved one another but weren't at all close. They were, as the UK saying goes, "as different as chalk from cheese." I asked Mark if he would pray over Bruce, if he would repent for his part of any division that existed between them, and if he would bless Bruce, especially in the areas where their personalities were so different. Mark prayed the most humble, earnest, insightful prayer.

In the next hours we also received multiple messages through social media. As people were praying for Bruce, they felt God showing them that unless they reconciled with someone in their lives, they would have no authority in praying for Bruce's healing. In other words, unless they played their role in healing the wounds in the Body of Christ, they would not see healing in Bruce's body. So throughout the night, we felt deeply grieved about the disunity in the Church across our nation and we prayed together in unity.

By the following night, Tuesday, we were still without any noticeable improvements in Bruce's body. As we continued to earnestly pray for a miracle, I was struck by the irony of the situation. 1 Corinthians 12 speaks of the gift of miracles. If I ever knew a man who I thought had a calling to operate in the gift of miracles, it was Bruce. But in order to operate in miracles, he first needed to receive a miracle.

I had a myriad of questions. Why is the gift of miracles not flourishing in the Canadian Church? If the Spirit of God gives the gift of miracles to individuals "as he wills" (1 Corinthians 12:11), then why isn't He doing it? Why is the gift of healing flowing at a trickle and the gift of miracles hardly at all? Lord, where have we grieved Your Holy Spirit? Where do we need to repent?

What would it take to see the Church across Canada genuinely full of the Holy Spirit—where all of His many graces and gifts and abilities and ministries are operative? We need it all! But there are things we have done that have grieved the Spirit and caused a disruption in the flow of graces He desires to bestow.

Sin doesn't simply evaporate. Sins from the past have a bearing on our present and future. They have consequences until heartfelt repentance is applied. Repentance says, "I have had a part in that sin, I have contributed to the things that are grieving the Spirit." True repentance means, "I have made the necessary efforts to understand where we went wrong, I take responsibility for it, and for my part, I'm committed to preventing that from happening again."

It was then that the Lord showed me that the gift of miracles had been used for self-aggrandizement and personal financial gain. This has grieved His Spirit.

Gifts from God are given with a distinct purpose in mind, and it is imperative that we hold them to that purpose. When the Church uses God's gifts for purposes other than God wills, the gifts can be suspended for a time.

So repentance must begin with me. Lord, where have I used the gift of miracles for wrongful purposes? Where did I hope that miracles would exalt *me* and not God alone? Have I allowed people to think that miracles were happening through me because there was something exceptional about me? Did I ever use miracle stories to bolster my image or to garnish financial support?

There is a teaching on financial "sowing and reaping" drawn from 2 Corinthians 9:6ff—some forms of it are healthy and Biblically sound, while others are concerning. I have heard it said in various places across Canada (I paraphrase), "It's important what soil you sow your seed into. Sow into our miracle ministry and you will receive your miracle." Try to find that sentiment in this passage of Scripture! I have also heard it preached (again I paraphrase), "Sow your money into our miracle ministry and reap the salvation or physical healing of a loved one." Beloved, these are very dangerous untruths with serious consequences.

When we are bringing together money and miracles, great care must be taken. There are right ways for churches and ministries to gain financial support, but there are certainly wrong ways. Ask Gehazi, servant of Elisha the prophet, who was made leprous for going about this the wrong way (2 Kings 5). Ananias and Sapphira were not straightforward about financial matters and it was considered lying to the Holy Spirit (Acts 5:1ff). The consequences were devastating. Simon tried to combine money and the ministry of the Spirit in the wrong way and was sternly rebuked. "May your silver perish with you, because you thought you could obtain the gift of God with money...Repent, therefore, of this wickedness of yours, and pray to the Lord that, if possible, the intent of your heart may be forgiven you" (Acts 8:14ff).

That night we asked God to forgive us for every instance where we misused the gift of miracles and especially where we used it to aggrandize ourselves or to profit from it financially.

We cherished the nurse we had that night. We had an arrangement with her—if she gave us her professional opinion on what Bruce's body needed throughout the evening, we would pray in one miracle at a time. So, if she said that what Bruce most needed was for his blood pressure to stabilize so that his heart rate would drop from its dangerous heights, we would send a message out to everyone praying. As his vitals responded positively, we would relay that message back to all the people praying. Sometimes we could hear the cheers coming from the ICU waiting room! People were so excited to see their prayers making a difference. That same nurse later told her fellow staff, "Don't ask those people to leave. Something happens when they pray. Bruce needs them."

This was non-prescriptive prayer. We had to let God do miracles His way. And He was. His way, in this instance, was one step at a time. Like a stalk of corn, faith began to grow in the thousands who prayed. The miracle of the blood pressure stats was like a seed. Next came the stalk, the leaves, the flower, and finally the fruit (Mark 4:26-29). The miracles continued to happen, one after the other. It was the Lord's doing and marvellous to behold!

A couple days later, one of the nurses came to me saying, "I've never seen such love in a community. I used to be a skeptic. I used to believe only in medicine, but what I have watched in these days is beginning to change my mind. I saw miracles in this room. When you guys are praying over that guy's body, something is happening." Faith was growing in her heart. And also in ours.

We genuinely believed that it was not yet God's time for Bruce to depart this life. If it was Bruce's time, then faith should have been exercised differently, but this felt like the opposite. God had given and continued to give a gift of faith to a growing number of people that they might fervently contend for Bruce's life. People sent messages from all over the world attesting to this. It was an exciting stage where we felt we were all part of seeing God do a great miracle before our eyes. But that faith would still be tested. That test came on Good Friday.

Good Friday was a far from easy day. When I came into Bruce's room that day, it was full of death and the fear of death. It was on people's faces. Trying to focus and pray, I could even hear voices masquerading as God's voice, saying, "You all fought so well but it's now time to let Bruce go." My head was spinning, trying to discern the truth. And then I actually stopped, like someone would screech a car to a halt, and said, "That's not right. That's not God. That's counterfeit." I considered the victory of the cross and said to death, "You cannot have him."

Bruce's father took me aside and asked, "Will he be okay?" I replied with a quiet assurance, "Yes, he will be okay." This must only have confirmed what he expected. What followed was one of the most beautiful sights I witnessed through all those days. That Good Friday, when death seemed so imminent and the halls of the hospital were literally lined with concerned people, Bruce's father went about, in the most precious fatherly way, strengthening everyone. A man who could have lost so much and had nothing to hang onto but faith in God proved that that was sufficient. Bruce pulled through. But that was not an easy day.

This entire story had what seemed like the strangest twists of irony, which was in reality the incredible wisdom of God playing out. Here is a man who longs to see prayer increase in our country, and with his life hanging in the balance he is the cause of a nationwide increase in prayer. This man longs to see the miraculous power of God restored to the church, but no one would have guessed that it was his need for a miracle that acted like a catalyst toward that end. That he would come so near to dying on the day Jesus overcame death—Good Friday. And that God would speak to His (spiritual) Body by means of a (physical human) body—a message to the big picture contained in the small picture. None of us could have scripted any of this.

Moses' burning bush is an occasion very similar to this. It was an individual experience that foreshadowed a national one. Exodus 3 must be read together with Exodus 19. In the first instance, Moses has a private experience of God's holy fire. In the second instance, Moses leads his nation to the foot of a mountain that burned with holy fire. The private experience contained embryonically the public national experience. Moses had to meet God in a certain way himself before he could lead his nation into the same. God worked something *into* Moses in the first experience, and God worked something *through* Moses in the second. The one made possible the other. The micro preceded the macro.

Bruce's illness had the same quality, and it was undoubtedly producing something in all of us. Persevering at prayer was producing the character of Jesus in us and thereby restoring true hope to us. We were daring to believe again that Jesus' authority really works and can be effectively exercised through His Church in our nation. Hope felt good.

The Church of Jesus has what it takes to take our place in this nation, but we are in the first steps of learning what that means. What was happening in Bruce was a microcosm—a small picture portraying vividly a larger one. The Body of Christ in our nation, although it has huge potential, has been weakened through toxins—like disunity and a misuse of the gifts of the Holy Spirit, to mention a few. It is sleeping, but it will rise. It is weak, but it will be strong again.

Many who hear this story may also find themselves longing to see the restoration of all things. To such pastors and leaders, even in other countries, I would urge you to not be afraid to ask God some key questions: What has been lost to us? Are there gifts from heaven we have used wrongly? What do You require of us in order to be restored? What would it look like to properly represent Jesus Christ in our nation?

I would also caution you against looking for fast, cost-free solutions. For example, the dream that the Church would become a deeply loving, Christ-centred community is commendable. But there is no such thing as a quick, cost-free way to creating authentic community. That is in fact a contradiction in terms. The idea that somehow we're going to have some quick and easy way into loving community is simply a myth or, worse, a lie. Rather than looking for ways that are cost free, I urge us to look for ways that are costly. We pay most for what we value most. In the words of King David, "I will not offer...to the LORD my God that [which] cost me nothing" (2 Samuel 24:24). In every conceivable way pay the cost—with our time, our heart, our money, whatever—because the goal is utterly worth it. And when paying a cost no longer feels like a sacrifice but rather a joy, then love will have done its perfect work in us.

Some of our greatest joys in this story happened latest at night. At around 3:30 am every night, people seemed to need a break from the intensity of it all. We gathered in the ICU waiting room and started swapping stories: tales of faith and of life's most embarrassing moments ("Check this out..."). I'm sure we laughed harder than we ought to have just outside the ICU.

People stocked the waiting room with food and drink, and we would make this available to every grieving family there. On Good Friday there were in excess of 100 people in the hospital for Bruce. The hallways were lined with praying people. One nurse said with emotion, "I've never seen a community love like this." Meals were brought to the Merz home, for their family and visiting relatives, for the entire time he was in the hospital and days beyond. Oh, the time we spent together as a community, seeking God and loving one another! We were praying for one miracle (the restoring of Bruce's body) and God first gave us another—the restoring of love and unity in His Body!

Many who hear this story may find themselves in a position of lost hope. I returned to Canada in the spring of 2003 after living in the UK. That summer I was participating in city-wide Christian gatherings across the nation. I couldn't help but notice that there was an acute sense of diminished hope in people, and I remember saying to myself that if there were one verse of Scripture that best described what I was seeing, it would be, "Hope deferred makes the heart sick" (Proverbs 13:12). What was odd to me was that it was among some of the strongest faith people, the ones who had caught a vision of what God could do in a country, but change hadn't transpired either the way they thought or at the speed they thought, and they had become discouraged.

Many who hear this story may feel that same discouragement. As much as we want this story to help restore hope in you, we realize that it may first help you to recognize the hopelessness that is in you, just beneath the surface.

Loss is painful. When we love deeply, we will feel loss deeply. Whether that is the loss of a loved one, of a cherished dream, or a God promise, or a ministry, or the loss of hope itself. A thought for you to consider: what pushes painfulness (i.e., "it hurts") into hopelessness (i.e., "I'm finding it hard to believe again") is our skewed beliefs.

For example, losing a loved one is inherently painful. It is perfectly natural to hurt in this circumstance. However, seeing that loss against a bigger picture is part of where our healing is found. Knowing that our loved one did not die because of our unbelief.

The salvation we have through Christ ought to be understood properly. This salvation Jesus has made possible is spoken of in the Scripture in all three tenses. Some places emphasize that Christ *has* saved us (past tense), others that He is *still* saving us (present tense), and still others that we are *awaiting* salvation (future tense). One aspect of our salvation is perfectly and already accomplished (justification). Another aspect of our salvation occurs over time as we are being made more and more like Christ (sanctification). And the third aspect of our salvation lays before us—the salvation of our bodies (glorification), where we are given imperishable bodies (1 Corinthians 15:35) like Jesus' own resurrected body. It is only with this hope in mind that we can say, "Precious in the sight of the LORD is the death of his saints" (Psalm 116:15).

Therefore, when we cannot see the "preciousness" in the death of a Christian, we are missing something spectacular. When loved ones die, even if they die prematurely, we can still be assured that they have graduated to better things—the full and final realization of their salvation! The receiving of *everything* Christ died to give them! Their salvation has become complete.

Physical healings, even a Lazarus-style resurrection from the dead, are wonderful miracles! But they are still only pointing to something greater. We get physically healed and rightfully thank God, but it is only a matter of time until sickness or weakness befalls us again. However strong our faith may be or mighty our anointing is, we will not believe our way out of old age and its challenges. Rather, that healing is a foretaste of the great resurrection when we are given bodies that are not susceptible to sickness or degeneration. A healing in the present then ought to create in us hope for our future resurrection.

Lazarus was raised from the dead. But in time he died. Through his first (temporary) resurrection, he and his family received a revelation of a coming (permanent) resurrection. As Jesus said, "I am the resurrection and the life. Whoever believes in me, though he die, yet shall he live, and everyone who lives and believes in me shall never die" (John 11:25-26). Miracles and healings, sometimes referred to as "signs of the Kingdom," point us to that day when we will live fully in the Kingdom of God.

Others reading this story have not suffered so much through the death of a loved one as much as the death of a vision. Old Testament theologians use the phrase "prophetic telescoping" to explain how Old Testament prophets seem to prophesy the first and second coming of Christ in the same prophecy and yet didn't appear to understand the gap between those comings—the church age. It is like a powerful telescope that can look at a mountain range and see the peaks of the mountains but not what lies between those peaks.

Similarly, in our nation there have been Christian visionaries who have prophetically seen great things coming from God. They have seen rightly like one looking into the distant future through a telescope. But what they could not see was the time it would take for these things to be fulfilled and the trials we would have to endure in the meantime—trials that were not incidental to the promises but that actually prepared us for them. When things God promises us do not happen in the way we expected or in the time frame we expected, deep disappointment can occur.

I have the utmost respect for everyone who believed for great things from God for their families, for their communities, and for our nation. Like Abraham, they chose to believe something audacious. Abraham's faith was accounted to him as righteousness precisely because he believed the promise of God even thought it seemed almost ridiculous and he was powerless to fulfill it. We have had some prophetically irresponsible things done in our country that have caused people to expect the fulfillment of divine promises on a timetable that was not God's own. Broken heartedness abounds.

I want to stand in the gap and repent to these people for any way in which they were led into false expectations. But I also feel the need to tell them that their story is not done. Your exercise of faith was not in vain. Even though you have not yet seen the object of your faith, I see hope and redemption being restored. Perhaps Bruce's story may be instrumental in helping you understand your own story. May your longer-than-expected story (perseverance) produce something distinctly Christ-like in you (character), so that true God-given hope may be restored to you, a hope that does not disappoint and washes away all disappointment. What happened in Bruce's body is a sign of what will happen to the Body of Christ across this nation and what can happen across the world.

For more information on Bruce and Lara's story, including pictures and videos, please visit: www.whilehelaydying.com.

For more information on River of Life Church, including links to past sermons (audio and video), please visit: www.rolchurch.ca.

About the Authors

Bruce and Lara Merz are an ordinary couple who drive a mini-van, bandage knees, and go on and off diets from time to time. Bruce, formerly a pastor, spends much of his time presently as an educator and mathematics curriculum developer, yet still enjoys ministering and speaking here and there. He has a passion for seeing people exercise their God-given gifts and abilities in their everyday spheres of influence. Lara is a teacher and professional photographer who enjoys helping people see how beautiful they truly are, inside and out. She is a gifted communicator and loves to testify of the goodness of God. Together they are raising three small children and are active participants in their local church community in Lethbridge, Alberta.

Lightning Source UK Ltd.
Milton Keynes UK
UKOW05f0945181016

285532UK00014B/521/P